Clients Are from Earth, Attorneys Are from Law School

Insider Secrets for Partnering with Your
Attorney and Winning Your Legal Case

David Matteson, MPH, MURP, MS
John C. Peick, JD

BOOK PUBLISHERS NETWORK

Book Publishers Network
P.O. Box 2256
Bothell • WA • 98041
Ph • 425-483-3040
www.bookpublishersnetwork.com

10 9 8 7 6 5 4 3 2 1

Printed in the United States of America

LCCN   2012937702
ISBN   978-1-937454-35-7

Editor: Julie Scandora
Cover Designer: Laura Zugzda
Typographer: Stephanie Martindale

Disclaimer

This publication is designed to provide meaningful, pertinent, and authoritative information in regard to the subject matter covered. It is intended to educate and provoke discussions about the productive roles clients and attorneys must play to ensure the civil and criminal justice systems work as intended and designed. It is sold with the understanding that the publisher and authors are not engaged in rendering legal, medical, accounting, engineering, or any other professional services. If legal advice, medical advice, or any other expert assistance is required, the services of an appropriate professional should be sought. It is not possible, and neither the publisher nor authors intend, that this book should include all the information available on attorneys, dispute resolution, or the interplay of the client, attorney, and court system. Please search out and read as much as you can from all sources of information on the subjects covered herein.

CONTENTS

Chapter One
Lawsuit, Lien, or Legal Action: How to
    Hire a Lawyer to Get What You Want   1

Chapter Two
Manage Yourself and Your Issues   5

Chapter Three
Do You Need an Attorney?   21

Chapter Four
Rules of Engagement   35

Chapter Five
Why Attorneys and Clients Fail   43

Chapter Six
Selecting the Right Attorney   59

Chapter Seven
Communicating with Your Attorney   69

Chapter Eight
Understanding and Controlling
    Fees and Costs   83

Chapter Nine
Prepaid Legal Plans   111

Chapter Ten
Understanding the American
    Justice System   115

Appendices

Appendix A
Additional Reading   135

Appendix B
Sample Engagement Agreements   137

Appendix C
Internet Legal Resources   153

Appendix D
Internet Non-Legal Resources
for Consumers   157

Appendix E
State Bar Associations   159

Appendix F
Sample Litigation Plan   165

Appendix G
Deposition Guidelines   171

Appendix H
Glossary of Legal Terms   179

About the Authors   215

CHAPTER ONE

Lawsuit, Lien, or Legal Action: How to Hire a Lawyer to Get What You Want

GOALS

1. Working as a team
2. Moving from trenches to overview
3. Getting command of the situation

Getting What You Want

There are many self-help books on the market that, in one manner or another, suggest techniques to get what you want. These Machiavellian guides offer techniques that range from the seductive to blunter forms of coercion. Unfortunately, advocates of power-mongering generally fail to take into account the entire equation, most important, the people from whom your wants and needs will be satisfied. Of course, the manipulation of other people's emotions and actions may deliver short-term results, but sooner than later, your victims will figure out your tactics and become less responsive and even hostile to your desires.

Go Team vs. Win or Die

Taking a team orientation is an alternate and better approach to problem solving than "Win or Die." When you focus on motivating your teammates with a clear appreciation of their enlightened self-interest, you are more likely to engage them in mutual efforts toward a shared resolution. This guide, then, is for people who want to take control of their own legal affairs by effectively engaging the expertise and prowess of competent attorneys. When you and your attorney are an effective team, the solutions you will reach will be mutually satisfying.

Together, you exert maximum effort to achieve maximum results. This requires that you:

1. know the basics of the legal system
2. understand the constraints and forces that define an attorney's world
3. have clarity about your own role and intentions
4. manage the overall effort

Moving from Trenches to Overview

This field guide attempts to provide insight, guidance, and the rules of engagement so that you achieve maximum effort with your attorney. When you are done reading, you will know what to do and what not to do so that instead of alienating your attorney team members and making the whole job harder, you will be one of their most effective, organized, and satisfied clients. This guide will help you rise above the trenches of daily disputes and paperwork, see the ten-thousand-foot overview, and plan for success along the whole legal journey.

Back to Basics

Too often people are intimidated by situations requiring legal interactions, particularly when attorneys become involved. Our goal is to remove some of the mysteries and arm you with some basic skills and strategies, whether or not you've been involved in a legal action previously, to empower you to take charge of your own legal affairs. Being well prepared and well informed dramatically improves your ability to understand what you need and how to achieve your goals.

As Simple as Buying a Car?

Maybe your legal problem is filled with tangles and snarls of frustration, difficult personalities, misunderstandings, and disagreements. By comparison to complex legal scenarios, buying a car is easy. Nonetheless, in the car-buying scenario, you can save a great deal of money and stress by understanding (1) how dealers and salespeople are compensated, (2) the relationship between car dealers and manufacturers in terms of sales and warranties, (3) the negotiation dance, (4) how to do your homework and be prepared for the encounter, and (5) how to achieve the confidence and competence to express yourself intelligently and obtain the best deal for your acquisition. The same learning curve applies to legal disputes.

Competence and Confidence

It is the goal of this field guide to help the reader achieve a similar level of competence and confidence in dealing with your legal challenges and your legal team. This field guide is not an encyclopedia or comprehensive treatise on all legal problems or strategies. Instead, we are attempting to provide guidelines and exercises that train you in the process of legal problem solving and to encourage you to remain open to other learning opportunities and resources. The appendices included with this field guide will support you in making the most of the professional legal team you engage, ultimately so you get what you want. Command of the situation is within your grasp.

CHAPTER TWO

Manage Yourself and Your Issues

So You Think You Need an Attorney?

You hire an attorney because you need help to resolve a dispute, formalize an agreement, respond to a suit, comply with regulations, and all sorts of other reasons. It is often true that by the time you decide to ask for an attorney's help, the issue, whatever it is, has become complex, urgent, and often emotional. This can create considerable stress and confusion, which will directly affect your ability to effectively manage the attorney or other professionals you hire. Your effective management of the process will increase the odds of a successful outcome, keep the management tasks reasonable, and under your circumstances, allow you to achieve the greatest control and satisfaction possible.

Manage Thyself

To be successful, you must first manage yourself. Remember, this is YOUR issue, and the attorney, and anyone else you engage to help, is working for you. You have the responsibility to direct them. Naturally, you will rely upon their advice and expertise, but in the end, you should not surrender accountability for your issue to your attorney or anyone else. No one is going to care as much about you and your situation as you do. In the end, faced with realistic options, you are the one who has to decide what result is reasonable for you.

What's Your Story?

Each situation has its own story. Every story has its own setting, characters, plots, subplots, and emotional drama. Regardless of the genre of your story (divorce, dispute, personal injury, or business agreement), you must fully know your own story and how it fits into the rest of your life. Your intentions, grasp of the details, and ability to share them with others will greatly determine your team and your attorney's ability to craft your desired outcome.

As you will learn in the following chapters, an attorney is a highly specialized helper. Hiring an attorney can be an expensive and powerful undertaking. Take the time to know your story—it will be one of the best investments you make in a successful resolution. This chapter walks you through the process of documenting your story. It's one of the most important steps in generating a successful outcome to your legal action. Slow down, take your time, and follow the steps outlined on the next few pages. Your efforts will be rewarded later in the process, when this pre-work saves you time, energy, and costly effort.

The Cost of Clarity

But how, you are probably asking, does someone get clear about what happened? Well, frankly, clarity seldom blesses us at the beginning of things. It usually comes only as a consequence of engaging the issue. The more effectively we tackle what happened, deal with the events objectively, and imagine the various outcomes that are possible, the sooner we gain clarity about our story and our goals.

Back to School

Embrace the fact that your issue is going to be a learning experience, whether you asked to be a student or not. You are not going to know many of the answers until they are upon you. Expect that you will at some point say, "If only I'd known this sooner!" Unfortunately, you can't know anything any sooner than when you know it; beating yourself up for how you learn the lesson or how much it costs you is not very helpful.

Listen to the words of this adage, "It's not the experiences we have but what we learn from them that makes us the people we are." You get to choose how much of the lesson you take on and what you learn from it. There are no right or wrong answers. You are unique, and so is your situation, even though your situation may be similar to situations commonly experienced by others. Your attorney can guide you along the path as it applies to the legal aspects of your situation, but nine times out of ten, the legal aspects are only a part of your story.

Personal Injury, Personal Tragedy

It was supposed to be a fun trip for a mother and her adult daughter. The adult daughter, a mother of two little girls herself, wanted to go on a clothing-buying trip because she was moving to a larger city, getting a new job, and starting her life anew since a difficult period of marriage and divorce. They were travelling along a rural, two-lane road, weaving their way through the Cascade foothills.

Suddenly, from around a blind curve came a heavy-duty dump truck on the wrong side of the road. The truck crushed the passenger side of the car, killing the adult daughter. The mother, driving the vehicle, had serious injuries, including a broken arm and internal bleeding. The truck driver was unharmed. The horror for the driver mother of realizing her only daughter was dead was only compounded by realizing she was now responsible for two young orphans.

Unfortunately, in the name of frugality, this family had minimal $25,000/50,000 liability coverage and underinsured coverage. While most commercial trucking companies carry five million dollars of liability coverage, this trucking company was small, local, and not governed by Interstate Commerce Commission or USDOT rules, so it only had three hundred thousand dollars in coverage.

The surviving mother had over one hundred thousand dollars in medical bills before the treatment was over. She had to bury her daughter and would have to look after her granddaughters for a decade or more. Her granddaughters had lost their mother. Clearly the combined coverage was inadequate to pay out-of-pocket costs, plus compensating the granddaughters for the loss of their mother. The attorneys for the family tried vainly to find an engineering flaw in the road design or maintenance in order to bring in the county or state. No case could be made. The attorneys investigated whether the insurance broker for the trucking company might have failed to properly advise the company regarding its coverage. No case.

Eventually, the family accepted policy limits from the trucking company by way of structured annuities for the children and cash payments to the mother. The attorneys worked with providers and carriers so medical bills and subrogated liens of the health plans were negotiated down or waived.

The attorneys took care of the required Minor Settlement proceedings. When it was all over from a legal perspective, the family still had to face the future and move on.

Get Organized

This book will help you write your story, chapter by chapter, and you are largely in charge of how it develops. Sorting out the legal issues will be only a part of this experience. Accomplishing an objective perspective is not easy to do, especially when it is you and the things you care about that are in the middle of the issue. But you can do this, one step at a time.

Begin by getting organized. Buy a three-ring binder and a set of numbered tabs, 1-9. Create a table of contents as follows:

1. Mind maps
2. Summary of facts
3. Correspondence
4. Pleadings
5. Discovery
6. Research
7. Settlement
8. Journal
9. Calendar

The next several pages will guide you on what to put into each section.

Mind Maps

Sort out your story in your own mind. Get a large piece of paper and draw a mind map—a free-flowing diagram with words. Your central idea is the center of the map. Branches sprout out from it, each one holding concepts related to each other and to the main idea. Sub branches can grow from each main one. This method allows you to think in a different way and can help you generate more information than you would with a typical outline format..

This is a fun exercise, especially if you are a visual thinker. Purchase a flip chart or artist's sketchpad at your office supply store, or use Mind Meister or another online tool.

Draw your story. Don't worry about how it looks; that's why you bought a pad with many sheets of paper. This picture will develop, just as a writer produces a novel only after many drafts.

Use colored pens. Make arrows and lines. Show the players in your story and illustrate their relationships to each other.

Recording Your Story

Write about what happened as if you are writing to your best friend.

Think of someone you feel you can tell anything. This might be an old friend, a parent, someone from your church, anyone with whom you feel a confident connection. Imagine you are writing the person a letter, and he or she is interested in hearing every detail.

Tell all sides of your story. In your mind, there are always several perspectives that have a voice in your story. Share the facts, but share your feelings as well as the questions. Writing everything out has great power.

Or use a tape recorder and tell your story. This is the same technique as writing a letter to a close friend, but some people like to think out loud rather than put pen to paper. Choose the technique that is most comfortable to you.

In either case, after you record it, listen as you read it or play it back and add to it. Identify the essence of your story. It might be helpful to take notes and summarize for yourself those things in your story that are important and those things that seem extraneous.

Then invite people to review your drawing or read or listen to your story. Keep the group small, and be specific when you invite them, explaining that you are asking them to help you think about an issue that is important to you. You could meet over coffee or have them to your home for the evening. When they arrive, lay out the ground rules for your time together. For instance, you may ask them to first listen without interruption to your story. Their initial feedback might be to summarize back to you what they heard you say before they offer their opinions about what you said or their recommendations about what you should do.

The first goal is for you to be clear about your story. Have them help you with this aspect before soliciting their input about your next steps.

Keeping a Journal

Write a daily journal both to keep track of your story as it evolves and to record important points along the way.

Everyone approaches this proven technique a bit differently. Some like to record facts and figures. Some like to record every emotion of the day. In any approach, the thing to remember is this process is about getting ideas, thoughts, feelings, and frustrations out so you can be clearer about what's really important.

Your journal is for you. You won't be asked to defend your writing or correct the spelling and bad grammar. Keeping a journal is as much about expressing yourself in the moment as it might be about chronicling your journey through your legal adventure.

The keys to a successful journaling experience are simple:

1. Do it regularly. Make a date with yourself and keep it. Several times a week is good.

2. Write even if you don't feel like it or can't think of anything to say. Write, "I can't think of anything to say." Just keep writing, and you'll be surprised at what comes into your mind and where it takes you.

3. Do it for a minimum amount of time. Ten minutes is a good start.

What to Track

Once you've got your story documented and you are maintaining a written record of the events of your legal journey, other steps will help you keep the paperwork, communication, and management of the process organized. At a minimum, you should do the following:

1. Create and keep an organized file of ALL your activities associated with working on your issue.

2. Keep a calendar that tracks all phone calls, meetings, and other activities associated with working on your issue.

3. Write notes for every contact you make, and keep an accurate record of what decisions were made and who is responsible for agreed-upon action steps.

Remember, you are going to have to make sure that all the pieces come together. It's always better if you are on top of any deadlines and hearing dates that your attorney has to meet. Don't be embarrassed to call your attorney up and say, "I'm just calling to confirm that we're ready to meet this week's deadline." People, even attorneys, are generally more alert when they know someone else is keeping track of things.

Oversights and mistakes happen even with the most competent attorneys. Successful attorneys and their staff try the best they can to stay on top of events, but all of them depend on clients to back them up. It is ultimately up to you to make sure that your attorney and any other consultants engaged on your behalf give you what you need, when you need it.

Support Team

Recruit a support team. Pick one or a few friends with whom you feel comfortable and talk to them about the issue.

Your non-legal support team's role is not to give you advice. The team members' task is to be good listeners and help you be clear about what you're trying to accomplish, the resources at your disposal, and your strategy. Engage them in your story, and do this sooner rather than later. Not only can they help you think things through before you meet with your attorney, but also it is important that they already know your story if the unexpected happens and you need your support team to give you good perspective so you can make effective decisions. However, you must avoid sharing with your support team the specific information given to you by your attorneys which is confidential because by doing so, you destroy the attorney-client confidentiality privilege.

Other Professional Advisors

Excluding confidential attorney communications, keep other advisors and consultants informed, as well as others potentially affected by your issue and your decisions.

In many cases, the work your attorney is doing is only one part of the overall picture of your story. If it is a dispute, your attorney will help you handle the legal aspects of the conflict, but resolving legal points is often only a piece of the solution.

The underlying issue often continues to be a problem even after the legal points are behind you. You are the one that needs to continue to manage the problem and its implications in other aspects of your life. The work of your accountant, tax advisor, consultants, partners, and other business relationships may be affected by the progress and final result of your attorney's work.

Assuming you are not in a dissolution proceeding, your spouse, family members, and other close personal relationships should be kept up to date. This creates a two-way street of support. Keeping others appropriately informed improves the odds that any of their actions will be in support of your story and your intended happy ending. It also reduces the all-too-common phenomenon that occurs when people fail to keep others in the loop. Often, all kinds of unexpected complications arise that could have been avoided if people had only known.

Doing What Feels Right

Know that your story is about what feels right to you. It is seldom a linear, intellectual, or even rational story.

Be aware of the non-rational aspects of the story that are not so easily expressed. For example, even if you have hired an attorney to do something as uncomplicated as prepare a contract to memorialize an understanding where there is no disagreement, remember that this contract is an expression of your story. The attorney-client contract is an attempt to describe a sort of snapshot of a piece of your story, one that captures your intentions, hopes, emotions, fears, expectations, and all the other intangibles. Does it feel right? Pay attention to these feelings!

When you engage the legal system, many intangibles are left at the door because they are too difficult to standardize, codify, or measure. Nonetheless, they are as much a part of your story, if not more, than all the important-sounding language and trappings of the legal arena.

Remember that ultimately this process is about people. There is nothing intrinsically right about the law, although disregarding the law can have serious consequences.

Laws are a construct created by people to help give their relationships and interactions predictability and to reflect the intent of the norm. As those relationships and intentions change, so will the laws—albeit slowly. The point is one of your objectives is to keep legal rightness in proper perspective and balance with the other dynamics of your story.

Staying Reasonable

Be rational and realistic about your story. If your story is complex, it may be challenging to keep track of all the variables and their interplay. Don't be surprised or concerned if you have feelings of it being too difficult. This happens to even the most seasoned executive. These feelings are normal. Just keep doing your best. Even if you can only do some of it, you'll be better off than if you simply didn't try.

The Matrix

Below, there is a simple analytical tool that can help you be clearer about what is likely and what is possible. Use it as a guide, and on a large piece of paper, draw the matrix shown on Figure 1. Leave enough space for your entries.

FIGURE 1

Player	Player #1	Player #2	Player #3	Player #4
Issue				
Position				
Interest				
Influence				
Relationship				

From your story, list the principal characters or players. In your story, how do they define the issue? Ask them (or others) if possible or imagine as best you can how they would describe the issue. State these definitions as a question. What is the question, or questions, that each is trying to resolve? The person may not frame the issue question the same way as you do (which may or may not be a part of the problem). Give a separate line to each issue if a player has more than one. Be sure to include yourself in this matrix.

Next, what is the position that player has on that issue? In other words, what has that player declared as his answer to the issue question. For instance, if the issue of Player 1 is "What is the settlement value of this law suit?" his position may be $20,000. Next, list what the underlying interest is for that position. So, using our example, perhaps the underlying interest for Player 1 is, "I want to pay for the medical help I need."

The next row is where you describe the strengths and weaknesses of this player's influence. How able is he to assert his preferred solution, his position, on you?

The last row asks you to describe the nature of the relationship between this player and the others in your story. There is often great insight from examining the interplay between the various players in your story.

When you attempt to fill in this matrix you should pay particular attention to three kinds of data: (1) things you know for certain, (2) things you *think* you know and really should confirm, and (3) things about which you are ignorant. Use three different colored pens to fill out the matrix, identifying by color each of these three kinds of information.

If your matrix is full of data you know for certain, your analysis will likely be very reliable. If, however, your matrix is full of information you think you know or it has many blank cells where you are ignorant, then the reliability of your analysis will be very low.

You can enhance the utility of this matrix by adding additional rows, too. For instance, you might want to expand the "influence" row into several rows: strengths, weaknesses, finances, legal advantage, political advantage, etc. You may want to add other categories. Further, it is often helpful to break players into several columns. For instance, you may want separate columns for a particular player's lawyer, consultant, and CPA.

Doing the kinds of exercises described above are ways to clarify and track critical aspects of your story. Volumes can be written about the many permutations that can come into play in any particular story. Each person's story will be unique.

The key thing is to take responsibility and ownership for your own story. It is vital that you continually seek to clarify and manage your story. Sometimes it is useful to ask some of the following questions:

- Why is this issue in my life?
- What lesson shall I take away from this experience?
- What it the best thing that can come from this?
- What is the worst thing?
- What are the odds of either happening?
- What can I control and influence?
- What can't I control and influence?
- What are the barriers I have to conquer?
- What will I have to do to overcome them?
- Who will I add to my advisory team?

Once you are clear about your story and have committed to a system of managing it, you are in a more powerful position to manage your attorney.

To summarize, it's a simple, three-step strategy:

1. Know what a good outcome would feel like.

2. Describe the specific results you will see when you know you've reached a good outcome.

3. Establish the steps it will take to make it happen.

With this level of clarity, you can now better answer the key question, how much of what you're trying to achieve can be accomplished through a legal action? To what extent is it part of a larger issue that you're trying to resolve? Share the answers to these questions with your attorney.

Checklist and Reminders

☑ Am I clear about my story? Have I invested enough to give me a depth of clarity that allows my attorney to clearly evaluate the role of legal services in achieving my objectives?

☑ Do I have a full team in place? In addition to my attorney, do I have the additional consultants and advisors needed to achieve my objectives?

☑ Do I have a good support system in place? Do I have trusted people helping me track and assess the evolution of my story as it moves through the legal process? Am I getting good support to make objective and effective choices?

☑ Do I have an effective tracking and administrative system in place? Am I taking responsibility for managing my story? Am I keeping the accountability for my issue and being intentional and clear about what I expect from my attorney?

☑ Am I being clear in my communications with my attorney?

CHAPTER THREE

DO YOU NEED AN ATTORNEY?

GOALS

1. Know when to hire an attorney
2. Manage the attorney-client relationship for optimum results

Chasing Ambulances and Other Half-truths

Lawyers have always bemoaned their low public image, while the public creates a new crop of attorney jokes. Bar associations and concerned lawyers have sought to improve the public's perception through better professional discipline, People's Law Schools, speaker bureaus, and bar-association-sponsored grants to legal service and public service agencies. Lawyers are forever being reminded that good public images begin with their office practices. Nevertheless, the public's impression of attorneys remains low.

Free Law

Some believe the law is free. Since lawyers profit from controlling the levers of the law and its interpretation, the public may resent lawyers for controlling what is rightfully owned by the public. However, to believe as an underlying proposition that the law is free seems somewhat myopic in a world of staggering governmental taxes to maintain a civil society, civil rights marches, and the human blood spent in the name of freedom and protecting those very same laws from tyranny or anarchy.

The Layperson's Lawyer

Part of the problem is the failure of attorneys to adequately explain why society even needs lawyers. Too often the media coverage given to multimillion dollar verdicts, frivolous lawsuits, and criminals escaping justice through technicalities distorts the perception of what lawyers do on a day-to-day basis. These highlighted events obliterate the work thousands of lawyers do every day to assist the average layperson.

Lawyers work with the lay public in estate planning, property sales and purchases, occasional run-ins with the local constabulary, business contracts, and employee disputes. These same lawyers may also engage in more lofty enterprises, such as upholding your constitutional rights to liberty and freedom, preserving property rights for the poor as well as the rich, and assisting injured persons as they regain their financial and physical well-being.

Law as a Business

The expense of lawyers is another fertile area for public discontent. Certainly the hourly rates charged by lawyers, or the percentage of the recovery taken, can seem excessive. Yet few people appreciate the labor-intensive nature and high overhead of the practice of law. Most lawyers put in long hours. Thus, the basic business law firm operates on a business equation of: Revenue = hourly rate X number of hours billed. Law firms struggle with the same economic and non-economic concerns of any other business.

Law firms are not immune to shortfalls in receipts versus payables, staff salary and benefit demands, equipment costs, rent, and other escalating overhead items. The increasing computerization of the practice requires a heavy investment in equipment, maintenance, repair, upgrades, and training. Paralegals routinely earn forty to sixty-five thousand dollars per year on the West Coast and more in the East.

All of this expense flows out of the hourly rate or contingent fee. As a result, most lawyers see only a small fraction of their hourly rates or contingent fees in take-home pay. If money were the only motivation, most lawyers could make equal money with less stress in a number of other business fields.

Like any manufacturer or service provider, law firms must pay attention to quality-assurance protocols, training, personnel management, and other HR issues. Burn-out, staff turnover, and motivating high performers is just as challenging for law firms as for any other business.

What Are You Paying For?

So what are you paying for when you pay your lawyer's fee? Are you paying for the lawyer's education and experience? Partly. It's also true that people rarely appreciate the processes attorneys undertake to solve their client's problem.

When you ask the neighbor kid to mow your lawn, both of you have a fair idea of how much time and effort it takes and can arrive at a mutually agreeable price. When you come to your lawyer and ask to be defended in a lawsuit or negotiate a settlement, you probably have no idea and the lawyer only a sketchy idea of what amount of time and effort will be required.

The existence of other parties, their agenda, and their attorney's aggressiveness or willingness to settle only complicates the equation. What appears to be a manageable dispute can turn into an ugly morass. Financial expectations and projected results oftentimes go awry to everyone's chagrin or anger. The good news is that there are ways to manage your legal goals and budgets. We'll get to that in Chapter Eight: Understanding and Controlling Fees and Costs.

Knowing When to Use an Attorney

Neither this field guide, nor any well-intentioned series of books, can replace the lawyers in your life. Nor do we wish to give the impression that, upon absorbing the contents of this field guide, you can sally forth and take on the legal profession's finest in a pitched jury trial. However, hiring an attorney need not be an all-or-nothing proposition.

You can manage your legal affairs and simply call upon your lawyer for specific, time-restricted advice that you can then rely upon for your own negotiations. Prepaid legal plans provide an excellent source for this type of "ghost" lawyer, with unlimited telephone access in exchange for a monthly fee and/or discount rates on additional legal services. See Chapter Nine: Prepaid Legal Plans.

Choose a Trusted Family Attorney

If you do not have a trusted family attorney, you should talk to your friends and colleagues and get some recommendations. Then conduct interviews to see who matches your values, explains things clearly, and makes you comfortable. Pay attention to whether the attorney treats you fairly with respect to your questions, tries to steer you away from contacting other lawyers, or disparages other lawyers. By the same token, if the lawyer is honest, your personalities mesh, and he or she has experience but charges a relatively low fee, then go for it. You do not necessarily need the most expensive or flashiest attorney for most cases.

The other mental adjustment that many people have to make is that hiring an attorney is not an adversarial event. You may profit from the objective observations of your family or business attorney even in the most mundane of circumstances. Particularly when you observe the cost/benefit guidelines in this field guide, you should regard having a legal counsel on tap as cheap insurance. In short, preventive use of an attorney may save you considerable sums in the operation of your business or life. Be proactive in the use of attorneys!

Buying a Business

George was a high-level executive whose company, due to economic issues, offered him early retirement. Having time on his hands and not particularly interested in perfecting his golf handicap, George decided to buy a small business and pour his considerable business acumen into that project.

He hired a business broker to assist in his search. He reviewed a considerable number of deals and decided against them on the basis of his own cash flow analysis. He finally settled on buying an auto repair shop, which was 50 percent of an operation with shops in two adjacent suburban towns. Or so he thought. What he did not appreciate, and neither did his broker, was the seller of the repair shop was artificially inflating the sales of the second shop by sending cars from the other shop to the soon-to-be-sold shop for repairs.

When George viewed the shop, the lot was filled with cars. Unfortunately, the cars were there because the shop being retained by the seller had contract with insurance companies to handle their insureds' car repairs at a preferential rate. Once the sale closed, those cars stayed with the seller, and the buyer (George) suddenly found himself with an empty lot.

A year went by while George tried every marketing technique he could think of, all the while being told by the seller that he had screwed up the transition and that was the reason for the drop-off in incoming customers. Ultimately, George felt compelled to sue the seller, but the cost of prosecuting the claim and the uphill battle on proving his claim convinced him to settle for a reduction in debt to the seller. George ultimately was forced into bankruptcy but was able to hang onto the repair shop and is still struggling to make it a profitable business.

Where did George go wrong? First, he bought into a business with which he had no experience. Second, he relied upon business brokers who are more concerned with facilitating a sale than facilitating a denial of a deal. Due diligence was minimal. Third, he failed to require a thorough review of the operations and financials of the business, including preferred shop insurance contracts which would have alerted him to the potential drop-off in business once the seller exited that shop.

The Client Self-test

There are some people that believe themselves perfectly capable of representing their own interests. Whether this represents self-delusion or a clear-headed assessment of their skills can only be determined on a case-by-case and person-by-person basis. Most of us can handle some of the problems all the time and all the problems some of the time but not all of the problems all of the time.

The self-test (Figure 2) below may help you assess that ability. You could naturally slant this test to whatever desired result you want, but if you truly wish to understand your aptitude for taking on the job of an attorney, these questions should be answered honestly.

So take a moment and go through the test.

FIGURE 2

	Yes	Sometimes	No
Do I feel comfortable in confronting other people with my own views when I know they disagree with my perceptions?			
Do I enjoy verbal interchanges with strangers?			
Am I detail oriented?			
Am I an articulate speaker?			
Am I an effective writer?			
Am I a good negotiator?			
Do I understand the legal issues involved in the dispute?			
Am I able to do the legal research myself?			
Do I understand the relevant facts in the dispute?			
Can I take a detached and objective approach to solving this problem?			
Can I risk losing this dispute and still remain objective?			

	Yes	Sometimes	No
Can I afford to lose the amount at stake?			
Even if I win, will I receive enough money to offset my economic losses and the opportunity cost of the time necessary to collect any judgment?			
Do I have the necessary time to devote to resolution of this dispute?			
Will my existing job, career, or business not be jeopardized by my personal handling of this matter?			

Did you answer yes to every question? The further you fall from the highest possible "yes" score, the more you need to consider retaining an attorney. We have not tried to weight these questions, but obviously some of these questions will have a greater impact upon your life than others. In the final analysis, keep this adage in mind: "He who represents himself has an ass for an attorney and a fool for a client."

It's Time to Hire an Attorney

Life is filled with mishaps, blunders, and problems in areas such as criminal challenges, property, neighbors, pets, consumer, employment, business, personal, and family. Some typical issues are as follows:

Business

- Your customer wants a long-term contract, and you are uncertain about its terms.

- You are a consultant and need a template contract for services.

- Your product may have injured someone.

- Your products did not get to the customer on time.

- The truck carrying your products had an accident, and you need to know who pays.

- You are buying or selling your business.

- You want to give your employees a lie-detector or a drug test.

- You want to have your employees DNA tested to discover if there are any diseases in their future that will cause your medical insurance premiums to rise.

- You need a lease reviewed.

- You are acquiring a competitor's business.

- Your employees want to unionize.

- You want to have non-compete agreements with your employees.

- You need a patent for an invention or a copyright for software you have created.

Family

- Your six-year-old was injured on the daycare center playground.

- Your seventeen-year-old had an accident in your car.

- You threw a party, and one of the guests became intoxicated and caused an accident on the way home.

- You are buying or selling your home.

- Your neighbor just told you your fence is six inches on his property.

- A tree on your property just fell over and crushed the neighbor's classic 1966 Corvette.

- You are involved in an accident not your fault, but you cannot work for three weeks.

- You make some remarks at a party about one of your neighbors and later receive a letter from an attorney about defamation.

- One of your medical providers releases all of your medical records by mistake to the wrong recipient.

- A neighbor comes onto your property to return the mower, slips on your patio, and sues you.

- Your dog bites a neighbor child.

- Your sister and brother-in-law die without a will or appointed guardian for their minor children.

- Your parents die without a will, and you do not get along with your siblings.

- You want to adopt a child.

- You are terminated by your employer because you are too old or for other suspect reasons.

- Some drunk at a baseball game spills his drink down your back and, when you complain, hits you in the mouth.

- You spill incredibly hot coffee from a fast food restaurant into your lap while trying to open the lid and cause first-degree burns over your lower body.

- Your spouse wants a divorce.

- Your spouse is emotionally or physically abusing your children.

- You want to make a large charitable gift and need to know the tax consequences.

Criminal

- Your child is arrested for shoplifting.

- You are arrested for driving while intoxicated although you were only on prescription medication.

- The IRS is bringing criminal charges against a company for which you are the bookkeeper.

- You are being accused of stealing.

- You are an eyewitness to a robbery.

- Your daughter and her underage friends find your liquor cabinet unlocked and hold a party.

Consumer

- Your spouse dies, and the insurance carrier will not pay the life-insurance proceeds.

- A repairman refuses to correct shoddy work.

- A product you purchased is defective.

- You buy a new car and the next day have regrets and want to unwind the deal.

- Your spouse purchases an expensive item from a home solicitation, and you want to cancel it.

- Your car is erroneously repossessed.

- A creditor places false information in your credit report.

- Your landlord refuses to return your damage deposit.

- A business refuses to honor a pledge or guarantee.

- You are refused service at a restaurant or other public facility.

Checklists and Reminders

☑ Attorneys are skilled helpers who are operating both as professionals and as businesspersons in much the same way as you operate your own business or career.

☑ Working with an attorney requires your candid assessment of your needs and personality to insure you make the correct choice for an attorney.

☑ Know when the economic risk of not hiring an attorney exceeds the cost of retaining an attorney.

CHAPTER FOUR

RULES OF ENGAGEMENT

GOALS

1. Learn effective attorney management
2. Have patience to let the teamwork between attorney and client evolve over time

The Ten Rules of Engagement

1. Know What You Want
2. Be Organized and Do Your Homework
3. Be Honest
4. Be Realistic and Reasonable
5. Be Involved
6. Ignorance Is Not Bliss
7. Litigation Is Not the Best Policy
8. Accounting
9. Trust Your Attorney
10. Accept Responsibility

Know What You Want

An attorney is trained to analyze facts and applicable law, predict with reasonable certainty what actions can or cannot be taken within the parameters of the law, and when necessary, protect his or her client's interests in any legal forum. What an attorney is not trained to do is read minds. If you want to play Twenty Questions with the attorney while he or she tries to figure out what you want, have that checkbook ready.

It is important that you identify *all* of the factors that will make any resolution a successful one. This is not to say that all of your factors can be satisfied; indeed, some may not. Once you can identify the tangible and intangible factors in your perception of success, the attorney can begin to address each and every one of them. Otherwise, it is equivalent to expecting a fighter to go into the ring with one hand tied behind his or her back.

Be Organized and Do Your Homework

Whether you are planning on hiring an attorney on a contingent fee, flat rate, or hourly rate, you need to compile and make a copy of all the necessary paperwork that the attorney will need to review. If in doubt, copy it. Why? Because if you want the attorney to quickly assess your challenge and be able to advise you of available options, he or she must be informed. The attorney needs to know not only the good but also the bad about your matter. If time-consuming attempts are required for the attorney to get all the facts, your matter either becomes expensive (hourly rate) or delayed (contingent fee and flat fee).

A brief checklist of what you need to prepare:

1. A typed, legible, chronological narrative of the events leading up to the problem or issue requiring an attorney's intervention.

2. A list of persons and their addresses and phone numbers who have knowledge of the events or issues. Indicate what you expect these persons to know or tell the attorney if asked.

3. A list of your questions and what goals you want the attorney to accomplish.

4. A few days prior to the first meeting or substantive phone call with the attorney, mail or deliver all this documentation to the attorney.

While time consuming for you, this routine saves considerable time spent going over the material in the attorney's office and allows the attorney to do any preliminary research.

It is important for the attorney not only to understand the facts but also to understand your emotions, goals, and values as they relate to a successful resolution of the conflict. At the meeting, initially stick to the facts and issues to be addressed. As much as possible, discuss your emotional, moral, and spiritual concerns in as an organized manner as possible. Rambling discussions or cathartic explosions not only cost you money but also make the attorney wonder if the non-tangible needs completely outweigh the tangible.

Attorneys may be counselors in the sense they will listen and make suggestions about a course of action or conduct. However, when it comes to our real-life capacity to effect changes and resolve disputes, attorneys deal almost exclusively with the tangible. While there are causes of action, such as defamation or tort of outrage, which arise from someone making you feel bad, at the root of these claims are tangible actions or omissions which create tangible, objective damages for the claimant. You're as likely to be struck by lightning as to find exceptions to this reality.

At the same time, every experienced attorney realizes that resolving conflict to the satisfaction of the client is sometimes less a product of tangible results than the intangible rewards to the client. Even if a result is objectively minimal, if it satisfies the emotional, moral, or spiritual needs of the client, the client will leave the attorney with good feelings. On the other hand, as we have discussed elsewhere in this field guide, even when the client wins big, if the emotional, moral, and spiritual values are not resolved in the win, the client can go away angry, dissatisfied, and disgruntled over the civil justice system. The real-life limits of both the criminal and civil justice systems mean that the tangible rewards cannot always compensate the clients for the intangible costs the conflict has caused.

Be Honest

Your discussions with your attorney are confidential. Tell all the truth, not just what you think will make the attorney like you or think you have a good case. Sooner or later, the truth is going to come out. If the truth means you do not have a case, it is better to know it right away, instead of thousands of dollars later.

Be Realistic and Reasonable

With rare exceptions, courtrooms are not the place to campaign for some perceived moral imperative or to vindicate your honor. Disputes generally mean there are two sides to the perceived problem. When all the legal trappings are removed, what the judge or jury is going to do is seek a fair and just solution for *both sides*. Save yourself some money and try to settle the case on the same basis.

Reason is all too often forsaken for emotion when disputes arise. In many cases, lawyers are hired to do what clients cannot do themselves: The clients want to figuratively beat the living daylights out of the opponent. Clients have a right to insist that their attorney aggressively advance their interests. However, persistent hardball tactics and senseless, obstinate positions do little to solve any problem and only make your attorney rich.

There are times to stand firm and other times to compromise. Tell your attorney to use his or her professional judgment in deciding between the two. Otherwise, do not complain when your pit-bull lawyer sends you a second mortgage application along with the bill for his or her legal mayhem.

Be Involved

When you hire an attorney, you are delegating a task, not surrendering it. Insist on receiving copies of all the paperwork generated by and received by your attorney, and *read it*. If you do not understand it, ask for an explanation. Do not expect to be consulted on every procedural move made by the attorney in the case. However, as the case proceeds, ask the question: "What does this tactic or strategy do to resolve the problem or move the case forward?"

Face-to-face meetings with your attorney and the other side can often break logjams and misunderstandings. Do not waste your money on tactics or matters that are extraneous to your goals. Make your attorney justify tactics on a cost/benefit basis. If you can afford the time, attend all pre-trial depositions, motions, or hearings to get an understanding of the other side's positions and strengths.

Ignorance Is Not Bliss

It is sometimes amazing how many people take pride in not understanding even the rudiments of the law. The law from both a substantive and procedural standpoint permeates every walk of life and business. It defines the most basic relationships between people/people and people/property. There are plenty of books available that discuss basic legal concepts. Contrary to popular belief, a little legal knowledge goes a long way.

Litigation Is Not the Best Policy

There are three basic rules one must keep in mind about litigation.

1. Litigation is expensive.
2. No matter how much you spend, you can still lose.
3. No matter how much you win, you might not feel happy.

There are several non-litigation avenues available for dispute resolution that are cheaper, quicker, and less painful, such as mediation, arbitration, and rent-a-judge services. Explore these avenues before charging forward into the litigation morass.

Accounting

When you retain a lawyer, obtain a clear and written agreement on how and when the attorney is going to get paid. Attorneys charge by the hour (normally in tenths of an hour), on a contingent basis, or a flat fee. Most attorneys expect to be paid monthly.

Insist upon a narrative bill with a breakdown of the time spent or fee/cost assessed for each item or set of items. This breakdown is not to encourage you to call up and harangue the lawyer as to whether he really spent one-sixth of an hour on the phone. The breakdown allows you to spot duplicative work, billing errors (they happen to the best of us), and potentially excessive charges: A four-hour letter had better be good.

Pay any undisputed portion of the bill on time because nothing saps an attorney's motivation to excel for the client than the nagging thought he or she won't get paid. Running a law office costs a lot *more* money than people realize, and lawyers as a whole make *less* money than people imagine.

Trust Your Attorney

There is a crucial difference between client involvement in a case and client mistrust. If you knew everything the lawyer knows, you would not need to hire one. Your need to understand and stay involved with the case must be balanced with the need to appreciate the professional advice being tendered to you.

If you persist in second-guessing your attorney or always wondering what hidden motives lurk behind his or her recommendations or thinking he's just out to pad his own wallet, get another lawyer. If you can never find an attorney you trust, stay out of trouble.

Accept Responsibility

Last but not least, be capable of accepting responsibility for yourself. Not every misfortune that befalls you is someone's fault or responsibility. If you made a bad deal, it does not necessarily mean you were cheated.

Sometimes you have to correct a problem and simply absorb the loss yourself. There is such a thing as plain bad luck or simply a mistake or poor judgment on your part. Know it when you see it, and you might save yourself and others a lot of grief.

CHAPTER FIVE

Why Attorneys and Clients Fail

There are many reasons why attorneys and clients fail. Playing the blame game is a good way to escalate a disappointment or difficult news into a full-scale battle for the territory of being right. If you know the reasons for failure ahead of time, perhaps you can avoid them, or at least recognize them when they're happening and make a better decision.

Here are a few reasons for failure:

1. Breakdown in the relationship between client and attorney

2. Lack of competence

3. Lack of communication between client and attorney

4. Disparity between client expectations and realistic potential for results

5. Dishonesty on the part of the client or attorney

6. Events beyond your control

Breakdown in Relationship

No matter how much we want to gloss over the reality of the client-attorney relationship with professionalism and objective distance, even with corporations, we have a human relationship. Some individual person is the client, or in the case of a business entity, the face of the client, and some individual person is the attorney. How do these humans interact with one another to motivate each other to perform each one's appointed tasks in a manner that maximizes the effort and results for all concerned?

No Excuse for Abuse

We have all stood in line and witnessed some person abuse the teller, sales clerk, or other customer-service person because of some perceived slight, snub, or dissatisfaction. We have watched restaurant patrons, acting like spoiled connoisseurs of haute cuisine, send food or drink back with haughty contempt for the waitstaff or chefs who toiled over their culinary pleasure.

Do you ever wonder if they truly receive better service thereafter? Would it surprise you to learn that such customers and patrons are really sabotaging their ability to receive sincerely well-intentioned service from the very people upon whom they depend?

You Get More with Honey Than Vinegar

People should not be treated as welcome mats for overbearing or abusive treatment. By communicating your needs and messages simply and without abuse, you build motivation in others to help you get your needs met, instead of losing ground due to mean-spirited tactics.

Emotional control is another factor. The baby boomer generation extols the virtue of "letting it all hang out." Under the right circumstances, there may be some mental health benefit to that philosophy. However, from a relationship standpoint, control of your emotions is likely to prove more productive.

The Rambo Relationship

In business and professional matters, it seems counterproductive to inflict your emotions upon your team members or coworkers. We need to respect the emotions and well-being of others around us by not selfishly and irresponsibly burdening them with unwanted emotional tirades or outbursts.

Where did we ever get the idea that Rambo was a model for building long-term relationships with people? In the movies, Rambo was a disaffected war veteran that was a master of destruction. Is the person allowing him- or herself to run emotionally amok really building a constructive environment in which to nurture trust, friendship, and loyalty?

Tyrants Need Not Apply

Applied to the relationship between yourself and your attorney, what is the more beneficial relationship: (1) mutual trust, friendship, and loyalty or (2) mutual fear, paranoia, and resentment? (For those of you selecting #2, please put this field guide down, get your affairs in order, and get ready for one hell of a rough ride through life!)

So what kind of relationship do you want with your attorney? Although it varies with the type of practice, attorneys tend to operate in a triangular world of dealing with client expectations, legal-system limitations, and opposing-party demands. In litigation, these pressures can become enormous as the stakes for winning or losing climb exponentially with the size of the case. In the following true or false test, answer the following statements:

FIGURE 3

T F	Attorneys prefer apathetic clients that fail to become involved in their case.
T F	Attorneys prefer hostile clients that question every move they make.
T F	Attorneys prefer clients that are too busy or important to get involved in their case.
T F	Attorneys prefer clients that threaten them or throw emotional tantrums every time something does not meet their expectations.
T F	Attorneys respect clients that smile to their face and never question or complain, and then criticize them behind their backs.
T F	Attorneys prefer clients that concisely set forth their expectations, listen to their attorney's advice, and discuss the matters facing them with their legal counsel in a cooperative spirit to resolve the issue or crisis.

Did you give "true" for any of the first five statements? Or "false" for the last? If so, you are headed for a disastrous relationship with your attorney. Instead, treating your attorney with the same respect you expect will work wonders for a positive relationship—and outcome.

All You Need Is Love

Obviously we all want harmony in our relationships. Often the behavior that created the conflict in the first place must be set aside to achieve a resolution. The sooner that you come to terms with any behavior on your part that created your difficulties, the sooner you will find reasonable outcomes to your disagreement. If you can state your needs clearly and concisely and then cooperate to shape the conclusion, you and your attorney will be happy parties to a successful resolution of your problem.

We do not suggest that you slavishly adhere to what your attorney suggests. Far from it, we suggest you become truly involved in your matter. However, there are some simple rules of polite behavior that apply to your attorneys as much as anyone else. Some of these rules of engagement are set forth in Chapter Four.

Expect the Best

The most important concept is to trust your attorney or, if you don't, find a new one whom you do trust. If you want to motivate your attorney to maximum effort, express your needs and desires and expect the best. When those needs, desires, and expectations are expressed in a civil and businesslike manner with the simple understanding that you need an attorney more than any specific attorney needs you, your actions will make your attorney a loyal team player on your side, not an adversary perennially watching his back.

Lack of Competence

After a person has completed four years of college and three years of law school, passed the bar exam, and taken continuing education courses year after year, one would hope that the last thing you have to worry about is the competence of your attorney. In reality, your attorney's competence is determined by his or her field of expertise and the field of law involved in resolving your issue.

Attorneys graduate from law school with primarily a generalist overview of the law and with little or no experience in the practical aspects of resolving legal problems on the job. Then, more likely than not, they will embark upon a career which focuses on at least one, possibly several, but not all fields of law.

Trend toward Specialization

The sheer volume of laws on the books and the evolving, changing nature of the law itself compound this trend toward focus and specialization. After several years in one set of trenches, attorneys may have a general notion of what is happening in parallel trenches but have no detailed view of professional life and problem solving in other domains.

So through the door of this attorney's office comes Mr. Client with a problem outside the attorney's normal practice areas. Perhaps your case looks lucrative, or it has been a slow month, or he wants to branch out into another field of practice. Greed may overwhelm his good sense. He takes the case. Six months later you begin to wonder what is going on and discover to your horror that your attorney is wondering the same thing.

The Bodies of Second Lieutenants

It is here that the client remembers what his Marine Corps drill sergeant told him years ago, "The road to hell is paved with good intentions." (Actually, his second favorite saying was the road to hell was paved with the bodies of second lieutenants who forgot about security ... but that is another story.)

Although the attorney may be brilliant or experienced in a number of fields, once out of his or her field of knowledge and riding bravely forth into the unknown, the attorney puts both the client and attorney at risk. It makes for great war stories and potentially lousy results for clients.

The Non-learning Lawyer

Another variation of this competence problem is the lawyer who, in twenty years of practice, never met a continuing education course he or she liked. These are the folks that sit in continuing legal education seminars (CLE) and, instead of listening and reading the manuals, read the newspaper or play computer games. They claim CLE credits for having their posteriors in the chair, but nothing dents their gray matter.

Perhaps they lead professional lives of some isolation with no organization or group of colleagues to keep them alert to changes and new legal strategies. Guess what? They will miss opportunities, fail to press the right claim, or be intimidated by tactics which have been discredited by their colleagues. The client suffers.

Ask and Ye Shall Receive

The foregoing is not so much intellectual incompetence as experiential incompetence arising from inexperience or isolation. How does a client discover the limitations of the attorney?

Unless the attorney is lying, cheating, or stealing—a much worse problem—the answer is simple. You just ask. We explore some techniques and questions in this chapter.

Lack of Communication between Client and Attorney

Imagine sitting at the counsel table in a courtroom. The jury comes in, the court asks for their verdict, and the foreperson stands and states, "Guilty." Your attorney turns to you and says, "I knew we should have taken that plea offer." Your thought is "What plea offer?"

One of the most persistent complaints about attorneys is their failure to keep the client informed of their matter's status. Clients complain that they never hear from their attorneys, never see what the attorney is doing, or never know what is happening. Attorneys do not return phone calls or respond to letters. Most of the complaints are not only justified, but when attorneys fail to keep the client informed, they are also violating their own rules of professional conduct, which require the attorney to keep the client informed.

What Can You Do to Improve Communication?

First, stand up, take a big breath, and repeat several times: "I am not a mushroom!"

Second, when you hire an attorney, have a candid discussion over what communication levels you want. As a guide, the attorney should be sending you copies of what he or she receives and produces so you have a record of what occurs. The attorney should be prepared to give you periodic updates either verbally, by mail, or by email. Your calls should be returned within forty-eight hours from the date of the call by someone in the firm who is capable of answering the question or finding out the answer.

Beyond these simple requirements, the nature of the case will determine the amount and timing of communication. In a case which has highs and lows of activity, daily or weekly calls are a waste of time and money. In a case where negotiations are on-going, daily calls would be a minimum requirement.

The Communication Habit

Get in the habit of communicating by email, mail, or fax with your attorney when you have specific questions or requirements. Why? Because it creates something tangible in the attorney's hands to motivate and trigger a response. While it is important to remember the need to maintain a civil discourse, there is nothing wrong with having a paper trail for that discussion.

While preferences may vary from attorney to attorney, an email or fax is the best way to ask and answer questions. Clients tend to take some time to think through their questions, and as attorneys go through the email or fax, they can either answer it or refer the inquiry to a paralegal or associate who can find the answer and quickly get back to the client. The response times are much faster, and that speed makes clients feel, rightfully, that the attorney is trying to be attentive to their needs.

Ask for an Update

If you have not heard from your attorney for some time, contact him or her and ask for an update. Clients that wait impatiently for weeks on end, fuming and building resentments about their attorneys, are not doing anyone in the equation any favors. See our comments about telephone conferences in Chapter Seven.

We address actual attorney misconduct and what you can do to address it later in this chapter.

Disparity between Client Expectations and Realistic Potential for Results

Imagine a case where the clients are financially at risk and deeply emotional about the claims being made against them by ex-employees and ex-officers of the company. They repeatedly tell their attorney they will not pay a nickel to the other side to settle the case. When the attorney gives them a settlement offer from some of the employees that appears reasonable under the circumstances, the clients become enraged that the attorney would even consider suggesting they settle.

Many attorneys, particularly younger attorneys, might find their client's passion intimidating. The attorney may not persist in expressing his or her concerns. As you might imagine, in the preceding scenario, after a multi-week trial, the judge rules against the clients and imposes a low six-figure judgment, about ten times larger than the offer. The clients take their attorney aside after the ruling and berate him or her because had they known they had this kind of exposure, they would have settled. They fire the attorney and seek another attorney to champion an appeal. The first attorney loses the case, loses his or her clients, and will never forget the lesson.

The Baseball Bat of Truth

More experienced attorneys know that even if they have to use a baseball bat, they have an obligation to beat reality into their clients' skulls no matter how angry the clients become in hearing the unvarnished truth. By the same token, clients have to understand that killing the messenger is not productive. Taking this tough-love attitude may appear too conservative, but the clients should have no illusions about the range of scenarios facing them, depending on their chosen course of action.

Attorneys absolutely loathe surprises. As a client, your tolerance should be even lower because you pay the price for nasty surprises. On the other hand, you're not hiring your attorney to be your cheerleader. It might feel good to have your attorney be unabashedly your fan, but you are paying him or her to be your objective advocate. If you want a cheerleader, it would be cheaper to make a donation to your high school athletic department and ask the cheerleader squad to show up at your backyard for a barbeque.

The High Cost of Creative Marketing

Dr. Andrews (not his real name) was a respected physician and was experiencing some reduction in patient influx as the economy began to slow. A lot of his patients were losing their jobs and hence their insurance, and other patients were simply trying to cut back out-of-pocket expenses.

Dr. Andrews reviewed a great many marketing manuals and came to the conclusion he had to be innovative in terms of generating new patient intakes. So Dr. Andrews began advertising discount rates to uninsured patients. He solicited his existing patient base to refer patients to him, and they would receive gift certificates for their own medical care.

Suddenly, Dr. Andrews found himself the subject of an insurance company audit and investigation into his billing practices. That investigation escalated into an investigation by his state's medical quality assurance commission into his billing practices. Ultimately, Dr. Andrews spent thousands of dollars in the defense of his license and ability to practice because he failed to take into account the difference in marketing restrictions between health providers and the rest of the commercial world.

Having Reasonable Expectations

While you do not want to hire an attorney whose nickname is "Chicken Little," your attorney should be encouraged to provide a balanced assessment of your case, its strengths and weaknesses, and the range of possible outcomes. Outcomes can be possible, probable, highly improbable, but rarely certain beyond a doubt. While expressing outcome potentials in terms of percentages ("you have a 75-25 chance of winning") gives the process an unwarranted patina of scientific accuracy, using such percentages in gross terms can assist you to understand your chances. You need to know the different results that can occur. You may need to adjust your expectations to meet reality.

Dishonesty

Pronounced situations of dishonesty are limited, but unfortunately, there are attorneys that lack complete honesty in their dealings with clients. This level of dishonesty may involve fudging their credentials, padding their time, or misrepresenting their experience. More serious violations may involve serious over-billing, misrepresenting the status of a case to cover up attorney mistakes, prejudicing their client because of a real conflict of interest, or misapplication of funds placed into their trust accounts.

Clients need to make the distinction between an honest mistake and forms of dishonesty. Misunderstandings can occur between client and attorney because of communication lapses, forgetfulness on either side, and misjudgments. The practice of law remains as much an art as a science, and sometimes events do not play out as anticipated or planned by the attorneys.

Evidence may not materialize, witnesses may change their story, a client cannot corroborate what he or she believes to have happened in the case. In any of these situations, the attorney's original assessment may prove incorrect or unattainable. The foregoing scenarios are not signs of dishonesty, and they may not even be a mistake by the attorney.

What to Do If You Believe Your Attorney Has Engaged in Dishonest Acts

Get a second opinion from another lawyer that your friends recommend and trust; or call the local bar association to speak to someone on its ethics committee.

If your suspicions are confirmed, then find another lawyer to take over your case before firing the dishonest lawyer.

When you terminate the relationship with the prior attorney, get all of your records from that firm and transfer them to the new attorney. Check with your bar association to find out if the attorney can ethically charge you for making a copy and/ or retain the original and give you the copy. (See Appendix E.)

File a complaint with the local or state bar association about the dishonest conduct of the prior attorney.

Evaluate whether you have a malpractice claim against the prior attorney. Generally, malpractice cases are not worth the time and expense unless you have suffered tangible financial losses as a result of the attorney's dishonesty that exceed the cost of bringing an action.

Events beyond Your Control

As Forrest Gump in the movie by the same name told us, "[$#]it happens!" Unless your claim or case is resolved overnight, your success may be subject to any number of calamities, if nothing more than events arising from the passage of time.

A partial list of events that can affect your case:

- A key witness dies or moves without any forwarding address before a deposition is taken.

- A missing witness is found that completely and negatively alters your defense.

- The company you are suing goes into bankruptcy.

- The person you are suing has very limited insurance to cover your large economic and non-economic loss, leaving you not fully compensated.

- You are a self-employed sales representative and are temporarily disabled in an accident. You suffer a large loss of compensation because of your injuries, but a general economic turndown in your industry complicates your ability to prove loss of income was caused by the injury and not the economy.

- Your case will be tried in a county with much more conservative jury verdicts than your own home county.

- You acquire a business and lose some of the key personnel upon whom you were counting to stay.

- You negotiate a long-term materials contract only to discover one of your competitors has released a competitive product that will force you to alter your manufacturing process and not consume the negotiated materials.

- An accidental electrical fire destroys files and documents critical for the success of your case.

It is important to remember another one of Gump's observations when evaluating whether an attorney failed you as a client (which, after all, is the point of this chapter) or you were simply the victim of unanticipated fate: "Are we all simply feathers blowing in the wind?"

There are, naturally, means by which some of the calamities can be avoided. For instance, taking the depositions of witnesses early in the case can reduce the risk of lost or deceased witnesses. However, it will be substantially more expensive to take everyone's deposition early in a case if you are hoping to settle it. Having off-site caches for important documents, or computer back-up systems can eliminate document loss. You need to make these cost/benefit decisions in conjunction with your attorney.

What Can You Do to Prepare for Contingencies?

Plan the strategy for the case with your attorney, including the timing of depositions and other discovery with a discussion of the cost/benefit tradeoffs to be made.

Anticipate the loss of documents, etc. by creating backup copies or digital copies.

In your business dealings, discuss possible scenarios with your attorney regarding your business. In this fashion, the attorney should be better able to negotiate and draft a contract to handle such contingencies.

The risks of being injured by an uninsured or underinsured person can be reduced by appropriate levels of UM/UIM insurance, health coverage, and disability insurance.

Checklists and Reminders

- ☑ Pay attention to preserving both your professional and personal relationship with your attorney.

- ☑ Question your attorney to ensure he or she has the requisite experience and understanding of your problem so can competently handle it.

- ☑ Insist upon communication from your attorney, and reciprocate by keeping the attorney advised of events in your life that may impinge upon your case or matter.

- ☑ Control your expectations and do not be afraid to ask the parameters of any solution or resolution of your problem to keep your expectations realistic.

- ☑ Be alert to actions by your attorney that do not appear bona fide or honest. Remember: The attorney that will cheat for you will ultimately cheat you as well.

- ☑ Not everything in the world can be controlled by either you or your attorney, so be prepared for contingencies and philosophic about their occurrences.

CHAPTER SIX

SELECTING THE RIGHT ATTORNEY

GOALS

1. Understand the classifications of attorneys

2. Choose the kind of attorney you wish to retain

3. Identify specific selection and interview techniques

How to Find an Attorney

Based upon a study prepared for lawyers.com published by Martindale-Hubbell, Americans tend to spend more time researching the purchase of a major home appliance than retaining an attorney. While the finding might be surprising, people do spend a lot more time with their refrigerator than their attorneys, so perhaps it makes sense.

There are some interesting facts which emerge from the above study in terms of how and why Americans find, choose, and retain an attorney:

+ Of those polled, 75 percent rely on friends and family as their first choice in finding an attorney.

+ Yellow Pages are the second choice at 50 percent versus the Internet at 32 percent.

+ Although most believe expertise in a particular field is important in the selection process, women seem more concerned (62 percent) than men (54 percent).

+ Most, 77 percent, consider the amount of experience and type of clients and cases handled important factors in selection.

+ Of those polled, 88 percent believe that trust in the attorney and his or her skills is important. However, only 57 percent trust their attorney from the outset and many require some demonstration that trust is warranted.

+ Of the people polled, 57 percent indicated that everyone should have an attorney available in case they need one. *(Good reason to have a prepaid legal plan!)*

+ Almost all, 95 percent, indicate they would hire an attorney for a divorce.

+ And 86 percent indicate they would hire an attorney for a personal injury.

+ Men and women tend to hire attorneys on an equal basis, 70 percent and 66 percent respectively.

+ Of those who had worked with attorneys, 29 percent were extremely happy and 67 percent would retain the attorney again. Only 9 percent were dissatisfied with their choice

Where to Look

Consistent with the above survey results, the best method of finding a good lawyer is ask your friends, co-workers, and family for recommendations. They already experienced the attorney's personality, display of competence, and capacity to get the job done.

Some attorneys regard the Yellow Pages as a particularly powerful method of soliciting clients. Unfortunately from the client's standpoint, the Yellow Pages represent more about what attorneys are willing to spend for advertising than whether they would be a successful match for the client and their issues. As the above survey indicates, 50 percent of the survey's respondents select their attorneys through this medium.

Another method of finding a lawyer is through the Internet. There are dozens of websites dedicated to helping the general public find lawyers in a variety of fields. An excellent site is lawyers.com, a website promoted by Martindale-Hubbell, the long-time attorney directory and rating service.

If you belong to a prepaid legal service plan, the plan's attorneys generally can refer you to pre-approved panel attorneys to handle your case or matter.

Many law school libraries and county law libraries also maintain a "jury verdict" service, which tracks tort and business claims. Review the jury verdict reports; they generally list the attorneys for both sides. If an attorney successfully resolved a case similar to your own, then he or she should be placed on your list to contact.

Most state or local bar associations maintain lawyer referral programs, which have panels of attorneys who have selected various legal areas in which they accept referrals from the bar association program. Most, but not all, of the attorneys on these panels tend to be younger attorneys using the panel membership as a means to obtain clients and experience. Depending on the nature of your case, their age should not be a criterion. Personality and competence should be the deciding factors.

Research the Credentials of an Attorney

Call the state bar association and inquire if the attorney has any bar complaints, what the results of any investigations were, or if sanctions were imposed. Anyone can file a bar complaint, so the mere existence of a complaint history is not as important as what the complaints were about, who filed them, and the results of any investigations. State bar associations vary with respect to how much information they treat as public record. Do not be surprised if some states will not divulge without written requests or even subpoenas.

Go to your local legal library if you do not have Internet access, and check out Martindale-Hubbell's legal directory of attorneys. In the alphabetical listing of attorneys, you will find the rating of the attorney by Martindale-Hubbell. Ratings run from "unrated" to "CV," "BV," and "AV." These ratings are originated from polling other attorneys in the same geographic area or same practice area as the lawyer being rated. "AV" is the highest rating, and reflects the peer perception that the attorney is highly ethical and competent.

Two caveats are worth mentioning: First, polls cannot be strictly trusted because there is little control over who decides to respond or not respond. Second, Martindale-Hubbell does not make a big effort to rank or update their rankings for attorneys that do not pay to have their biographical information listed in their directories. Nevertheless, the directory is one good source of information about law firms in your area.

If you do have Internet access, check www.lawyers.com for Martindale-Hubbell's rankings and information on attorneys. You can also access attorney information at www.avvo.com where attorneys provide biographical information and clients can provide reviews.

Call the local Better Business Bureau and find out if any complaints have been filed. Most attorneys do not belong to BBB, but some feedback may have occurred.

Ask the attorney for a résumé in advance of interviewing him or her. Ask the attorney to provide you with a list of articles or publications that he or she has authored and copies of them, if available. What are you looking for in the résumé? The attorney's education is the least important factor. What has the attorney done in his or her career? What is the attorney's breadth of experience? What professional contributions has he or she made in terms of articles, books, or seminars?

Does the attorney belong to professional associations pertinent to his or her practice? For instance, does an estate planner belong to tax or estate planning organizations? Does a trial lawyer belong to and participate in trial-lawyer organizations? Membership in such organizations tends to mean the attorney is keeping up to date by staying involved in the intellectual ferment and education, which is largely the *raison d'être* of these organizations. While professional involvement does not guarantee competence, it is a reliable indicator.

Big Firm vs. Small Firm or Solo Attorney

The decision to use a big firm as opposed to a small firm has little to do with size and everything to do with expertise and resources. Traditionally, larger firms had the resources to have attorneys trained and skilled in a variety of esoteric legal areas and offered a comprehensive array of services to business and corporate clients.

Large firms tended to have large legal libraries that could rival county law libraries or law school offerings. Large firms tended to attract Fortune 500 and Fortune 1000 companies with vast legal needs requiring large numbers of associates and partners working away on their needs. Smaller firms could rarely match their investment in personnel or facilities to create such a comprehensive breadth of coverage.

A lot has changed over the years to level the playing field between small and large firms, but nothing has had more of an impact than the computer and Internet. Any attorney in any firm, no matter how large or small, has incredible access to legal source materials by way of CD-ROM materials or over the Internet through commercial outlets, like West Law Publishing or Lexis-Nexis, and public sites, such as FindLaw.

The production and management of documents has been largely computerized, and the day is not far away when attorneys shall operate in paperless or electronic office and court environments and create paper only for transactional matters, such as real estate closings and wills.

Most Valuable Players

Additionally, while large firms can still muster hundreds of lawyers under their banners, there has been considerable fragmentation and shifts in the legal profession over the last ten to fifteen years. Lawyers are much more likely to shift to another firm if they offer better compensation or better career opportunities. Entire departments of firms have been known to jump ship. Refugees from large firms often set up law-firm boutiques, focusing on special expertise and experience. The pool of talent is more diversified than twenty-five years ago.

How much such expertise and resources matter to you depends on the nature of your case. For instance, some large firms do not even have anyone in them to handle personal injury claims, particularly claims that are not catastrophic. Small business or solo professionals may not get much TLC from a large firm and find themselves relegated to young associates. Competence and expertise is no longer confined to large firms, so do not be afraid to look at solo attorneys and small law-firm boutiques for the attorney who fits your needs.

Know Your Class

Most legal challenges fall into two major classes, civil and criminal. Within the civil class are two major sub-classes, transactional and litigation. Transactional would tend to be contracts, leases, corporate issues, buying, and selling. Litigation is a form of dispute resolution and includes arbitration and mediation as forms of alternative dispute resolution (ADR).

Interviewing Your Attorney

When you hesitate to press an inquiry about an attorney's credentials and experience, you are simply laying yourself open for trouble. As always, however, there are a right and wrong approach to this inquiry. Questions that seem to suggest you already suspect the attorney is incompetent, stupid, or inexperienced are not going to endear you to the attorney and probably will build resistance to a candid exchange. The better approach is to ask non-judgmental questions designed to elicit information about the attorney.

Interview Your Friends

If you received the attorney's name from friends, then talk with them prior to your consultation. Did they have a good experience with an attorney? Did the attorney achieve their goals? Now that time has passed, was the result fair and realistic under the circumstances of the case? Would they use the attorney again for a similar case? For a different case? Did the attorney have any idiosyncrasies that may confuse you or act as a negative in the initial interview?

Make sure the attorney will provide you a free consultation for the purpose of interviewing and assessing if he or she is appropriate.

At the interview, you should ask the following questions:

- What experience does the attorney have in the particular type of problem or transaction you face?
- What difficulties, if any, would the attorney anticipate in the subject problem or transaction?
- What amount of time would be required to resolve the problem or complete the transaction?
- What will be the anticipated fees and costs associated with resolving the problem or completing the transaction?
- How will these fees and costs be computed?
- What arrangements need to be made to pay for these fees and costs, e.g., monthly, financing, installment basis from the attorney, etc.?
- If litigation is a potential consequence of the problem, what litigation, if any, has the attorney undertaken that deals with the particular type of problem?
- How many cases has the attorney actually brought to trial with a judge or jury in the general type of problem

you face? What results? For instance, the attorney may not have any trial experience in the specific problem you face but may have trial experience in similarly related problems.

- After explaining your expectations, what is the attorney's initial reaction to the reasonableness of such expectations? What is the basis for his or her reaction?

- Keeping these foregoing questions in mind, what is the strategy and tactics the attorney expects to deploy in this type of case?

- What is the attorney's current workload and how much time does the attorney have available to attend to your matter or case?

- What deadlines should the attorney and client agree upon to ensure work is completed on a timely basis?

- What case management programs does the attorney use in staying on top of his or her cases?

- What other software does the attorney use to produce his or her written materials, and what effect, if any, does he or she anticipate such productivity software will have on the time spent on this case?

- Who else will work on this case with your attorney in the firm? What are their credentials and experience? What are their billable rates? Is there ever an occasion when a lower-rate person does the work and it is billed as if performed by a higher-rate person in the firm? What is the firm's policy in this regard?

- Without discussing exact dollar amounts, how are partners, associates, and paralegals compensated? Are partners, associates, or paralegals rewarded for achieving certain billable hour goals? What procedures or protections does the firm have to ensure the accuracy of billing charges?

- What determines if work performed by a partner, associate, or paralegal is billable? Is there any policy regarding the nature of the work or value to the client for the work?

- Is there any differentiation in the billing rate used for research, travel, or other less intensive activities?

- If the attorney uses computer assisted legal research tools, what are the charges or surcharges to the client?

- Is there any surcharge for costs related to outside vendors or internal costs of the firm, such as photocopies, etc.?

Checklist and Reminders

☑ The best source of a recommendation for an attorney is your friends and colleagues with personal experience with attorneys.

☑ Do your homework with respect to getting information about the attorneys you intend to interview.

☑ Do not be afraid to ask attorneys about their experience with, and attitudes about, your case.

☑ In your interview, attempt to obtain (keeping in mind limited information) a candid discussion about your case.

☑ Select an attorney on (a) competence, (b) personality match, and (c) range of expense to engage.

☑ In the final analysis, does the attorney want you as a client, and do you want the attorney to represent you?

CHAPTER SEVEN

COMMUNICATING WITH YOUR ATTORNEY

GOALS

1. Understand how attorneys communicate
2. Keep client-attorney communication channels open
3. Ensure your needs are understood and met

The Goal of Communication

Communication may be defined as (1) an act or instance of transmitting, (2) information communicated, (3) a verbal or written message, (4) **a process by which information is exchanged between individuals through a common system of symbols, signs, or behavior,** (5) personal rapport.

Understanding may be defined as (1) a mental grasp, (2) the power of comprehending, (3) the capacity to apprehend general relations of particulars,

(4) **the power to make experience intelligible by applying concepts and categories.**

When you visit an attorney in the United States, unless you specifically select an attorney that is bilingual or multilingual, you will be speaking English. However, even if you are speaking Spanish, Russian, or some other mutually shared language, communication with an attorney may breakdown if it doesn't involve **a common system of symbols, signs, or behavior.** There are expectations and styles of communication that can get in the way of understanding each other.

Objective Distance

From day one of law school, law students are constantly bombarded with instructions for their pending professional careers. Behaving ethically is number one, but not far behind is maintaining objectivity when representing a client. "Objectivity" means a lawyer is able to view the facts of a given case or claim without emotion or conflicting interests. To the client, a lawyer's objectivity often appears to be apathy at best and obnoxious disloyalty at worst. When lawyers practice objectivity, the common client response is, "Whose side are you on?"

However, it is the objectivity of the attorney that ultimately protects the client from taking on cases that are without merit or defending cases that should be acknowledged as a liability and settled. Clients may not always want to hear what their attorneys have to say. Their advice may be painful from an emotional, financial, or career standpoint. However, what is the alternative?

If you hire a cheerleader that praises your case and stands at the sidelines exhorting the crowd to cheer for your team, no matter how overmatched your team may be, who in the end will suffer the loss—the player lying shattered and exhausted on the field or the cheerleader going out for a post-game party?

There is nothing wrong with an attorney expressing remorse for a client's situation or being compassionate about a client's predicament or loss. However, such compassion or remorse should not preclude an attorney from expressing his or her true professional opinion about the merits of any case or claim. The client that punishes an attorney for such expressions of opinion risks far more than an unpleasant session with his or her legal advisors.

Simplicity vs. Complexity

KISS (Keep It Short and Simple) is currently in vogue in our modern society. The KISS philosophy is a necessary antidote to unnecessary bureaucratic layers, senseless procedures, and mindless behaviors that flow from tradition and not modern need.

However, KISS can sometimes lead to an overly simplistic view of legal issues. For instance, a consumer reads an ad in the paper regarding the discount sale of merchandise on easy credit, with no interest charges. The consumer then proceeds to purchase the item. Five weeks later the consumer has two problems—the item does not work any longer and the finance company to which the contract to purchase was assigned has sent a dunning notice that a payment is overdue. The consumer soon learns that "no interest" is not the same as "no payment," and is politely pointed to the fine print in the reverse side of the contract, which he never read.

To the consumer, it is fairly simple: He just got screwed.

To the attorney, you have issues pertaining to contracts of adhesion, false or deceptive trade practices, false or deceptive advertising, issues regarding defenses against holders in due course, implied and express warranties, etc. Even if the law is clear on these issues, there are evidentiary issues on the actual representations made and their actual falsity or inaccuracy. There are presumptions that signing an unread contract still binds you and that ignorance of the law is no excuse.

How the client's case fares will depend on how the evidence is presented, the nature and competency of the fact-finder (judge or jury), and how the respective parties demonstrate their credibility to the fact-finder. Does all of this sound simple? If you think it is unnecessarily complex, place yourself as the seller in this scenario and imagine how your interests would be affected by a process where the result was based on an irrefutable presumption of the consumer's simple belief he was screwed. Is that the system you, as a seller, would envision as being in your best interest? Simplicity is a delightful goal. Complexity is more often the necessary reality.

Cases can often be analyzed with the following list of issues:

- What are the facts?
- What is the law?
- Where, who, and what are the evidence of the foregoing facts?
- Who is the fact-finder?
- What is the competency of the fact-finder, relative to the issues in the case?
- How will these facts be presented?
- What will be the credibility of the factual presenters?
- What will be the likely result?

- ◆ If the result is a judgment or order, how will that result be enforced, e.g., by obeying the order or collecting a judgment?

Keeping this list in mind, how could a client expect a case's resolution uniformly to be simple?

Nevertheless, a constant source of miscommunication and misunderstanding between attorneys and their clients is the attorney's failure to work with the client to reach an agreement around the underlying complexities of the case. The attorney is busy trying to win so the client is largely left in the dark and expected to wait stoically until the attorney brings home the proverbial bacon.

The intelligent and questioning client is rarely regarded as a nuisance unless the attorney is dropping the ball. On the contrary, the client who constantly whines about simplicity and the unbeatable nature of his or her case becomes an incredible nuisance to most attorneys. Communication and understanding is quickly lost.

Legalese vs. Plain English

The professor of a contract class asked one of his better students, "If you were to give someone an orange, how would you go about it?"

The student replied, "Here's an orange."

The professor was appalled. "No! No! Think like a lawyer!"

The student then replied, "Okay. I'd tell him, 'I hereby give and convey to you all and singular, my estate and

> *interests, rights, claim, title, claim and advantages of and in, said orange, together with all its rind, juice, pulp, and seeds, and all rights and advantages with full power to bite, cut, freeze, and otherwise eat the same or give the same away with and without the pulp, juice, rind, and seeds, anything hereinbefore or hereinafter or in any deed or deeds, instruments of what nature or kind whatsoever to the contrary in anywise notwithstanding …'"*

Comics invariably get a laugh by taking a common problem and exaggerating it to the point of hilarious distortion. The foregoing piece is humorous because it does register with people that find legalese unnecessarily verbose and complicated. Obviously, plain English would be an improvement in most legal drafting.

However, there must be a realization that plain English is not the same thing as simple English. Shorter sentences, less jargon, and less irrelevant boilerplate would be an improvement. However, trying to make legal drafting universally understood by someone with an eighth-grade education will ultimately backfire. Why? Because while plain English deals with word choice and sentence structure, it has no effect whatsoever in simplifying the truly complex challenges which life, business, and society can create.

If you were to make a gift of one orange, then telling someone, "Here's an orange," will do the job. Assume you are an orchard grower entering into an agreement to sell your ultimate orange crop to a fruit drink distributor. Will it be sufficient to say, "Grower will sell and buyer will purchase all Grower's oranges when they ripen"? Will this simple language cover the following scenarios?

- ◆ The crop suffers from blight and has to be destroyed. Do you have to find replacement oranges for the buyer?

- ◆ A labor strike occurs, and no union pickers will work. Do you have to hire more expensive scab labor to get the crop in the door?

- ◆ In your verbal discussions with the buyer, he or she anticipated receiving ten thousand pounds of oranges from your orchard. You only deliver eight thousand pounds. Do you have some liability?

- ◆ You spray your oranges with an insecticide that is later determined to cause cancer in lab rats. The buyer decides not to follow through with the purchase of your oranges. Can you enforce the agreement?

- ◆ The oranges are being trucked to the buyer, and an accident occurs. The oranges are scattered all over the highway. Those oranges that are not turned to oily pulp by passing cars and trucks are eaten by Everglades alligators. Does the purchaser still have to pay you for the oranges? Who was at risk for the shipment?

Fortunately for the parties, even in the absence of appropriate language, some of these issues can be answered by referring to the prior history between the buyer and seller (course of dealing) or by referring to the sales provisions of the Uniform Commercial Code (UCC).

However, you will probably need to hire an attorney to sort out your obligations, and it may have been cheaper to have a complete, yet plain-English agreement that anticipated contingencies and provided a remedy for dealing with such issues.

There is nothing wrong on insisting that your attorney use plain English, but do not insist that the attorney oversimplify what most would consider a complex or critical transaction. Such insistence on the KISS approach will invariably return to bite you.

Where Are We?

Mike and Pat decided to take a helium balloon ride. Unfortunately, they did not pay attention to the weather and were caught up in a violent storm. For several days, they blew around with the prevailing winds. When the storm abated, they found themselves drifting over what appeared to be little farms with large houses. They spotted a gentlemen strolling down one of the roads and called down to him. "Where are we, sir?"

The gentlemen stopped, looked up, pondered his response, and replied "In a balloon."

Mike and Pat drifted out of earshot. Mike turned to Pat and stated, "That gentlemen was an attorney."

"How could you tell?" replied Mike.

"Because what he said was true, concise, and not worth a damn!"

Ask the Right Questions

You need to ask the right questions in order to get answers pertinent to your problem. Notice we did not say, "to get the right answers," because what you perceive to be the right answer may have no relationship to reality.

"But I do not know the right questions to ask," you plead. Let me share a dirty little secret. At first exposure to a case, an attorney may not know all the right questions either. It takes a thorough understanding of the facts of the case and a command of the specific legal issues to know the right questions and pertinent answers. A candid and open discussion with the attorney will help both of you begin to understand the questions that bear upon the case.

"But I do not want to appear stupid in front of the attorney." What is more stupid, asking the attorney to explain the concepts bearing on your problem or nodding your head to give the false impression that you understand what he or she is trying to tell you? Is it any wonder in the latter case why communication breaks down between attorneys and their clients?

Absolutely no person knows all the answers to all possible questions. So relax. You are hiring the attorney presumably to take advantage of his or her specialized knowledge. So ask questions until you understand what is going on in your case. If the attorney loses patience with this educational quest, find another attorney that appreciates his or her obligation to have a client that understands the case.

We say this with one caveat: Asking sufficient questions to gain understanding is fine; asking the same question in different ways over and over, hoping to get the attorney to give you the answer you want, is a waste of everyone's time, including yours.

The Telephone Conference

Mr. Attorney is working on a lengthy brief for Client A. His receptionist buzzes him and tells him Client Z is on the phone. He picks up the phone, and after some pleasantries, the client starts asking specific, detailed questions about the client's case, requiring a review of pros and cons, and evaluation of fact and law. What is wrong with this picture?

Without a lot of luck, how is the attorney supposed to switch gears away from the brief, remember all the details of Client Z's file without having it before him, and respond to these questions? What is Client Z's expectation of the telephone conference? If the attorney deflects the questions or defers an answer, when will he have time to do the research and get back to Client Z in a manner sufficiently timely to satisfy Client Z? If he tries to answer the questions as best he can, will the generality of the answers offend or anger Client Z or, worse, mislead the client regarding the status of the case?

Is there a way to avoid this problem? All Client Z needs to do is alert the attorney to the questions in advance so the necessary research or thought can be processed before the client calls. In short, if the client does her homework (preparing questions) in advance of the conference, the telephone meeting will go more smoothly and be more productive. In essence, a telephone conference should be treated the same as a meeting. Few clients simply drop in to an attorney's office and expect to see him, much less find him prepared to discuss a case in detail. So why is a telephone conference any different?

The Communication Commitment

The guidelines in Figure 4 are not exclusive and are not listed in any particular order of importance. These guidelines simply acknowledge the respective obligations of both the attorney and client to ensure real communication exists in their relationship. These reciprocal obligations will go a long way towards improving communication between attorney and client.

FIGURE 4

ATTORNEY'S COMMITMENT	CLIENT'S RECIPROCAL OBLIGATION
The attorney will keep the client informed of developments in the case or matter.	The client will respond to inquiries from the attorney as soon as possible, depending upon the inquiry or information requested. The client will also keep the attorney advised if the mailing address, phone number, or email address changes during the course of the matter or case.
The attorney will supply the client with copies of all documents created by the attorney.	The client will read all documents provided by the attorney and call, write, or email if he or she does not understand the documents or if he or she spots errors.
The attorney will supply the client with copies of all documents received by the attorney.	The client will read all documents provided by the attorney and call, write, or email if he or she does not understand the documents or if he or she spots errors.
Absent an emergency, the attorney or someone on his or her staff will return a phone call or email from a client within twenty-four to thirty-six hours.	A client will not make multiple calls unless the situation is an emergency, in which case, the client should speak to someone else in the firm to get a response.

ATTORNEY'S COMMITMENT	CLIENT'S RECIPROCAL OBLIGATION
The attorney or someone on his or her staff will respond to written inquiries from the client as soon as reasonably possible, considering the nature of the inquiry and materials to be reviewed.	In the absence of an emergency, the client must realize that the attorney will not drop everything else to read over materials supplied by the client, and a reasonable time period may be required for such analysis and response.
The attorney will take the necessary time to educate the client about his or her claim and case.	The client will listen to the explanations, do the homework, and keep an open mind with respect to the information being provided. Most important, the client will not kill the messenger.
The attorney will never tell a client that he or she is not the attorney's only client since, for the client, it is probably his or her only case.	A client will appreciate he or she is not the attorney's only client and, absent an emergency, will understand that scheduling work assignments can take some time.
An attorney will not overcommit to produce work when it is unlikely to get done in time. Honest assessments of available time are the best policy.	The client will not create artificial time lines, hoping to produce work more quickly. Honesty is the best policy.

Checklists and Reminders

☑ Communication requires the transfer of understanding and not simply an exchange of words.

☑ An attorney doing his or her job will try to maintain an objective distance from the problem. Do not treat this objective distance as apathy or lack of compassion.

☑ Simplicity is a desirable goal, but it should not be utilized in a fashion that ignores the complexities of life or transactions.

☑ Asking the right question requires accepting the true answer, not necessarily the desired answer.

CHAPTER EIGHT

UNDERSTANDING AND CONTROLLING FEES AND COSTS

GOALS

1. Understand how attorneys bill for service
2. Review typical costs
3. Avoid billing abuses
4. Maintain control over the attorney's time charges

Factors in Determining Attorney Fees

Attorneys are bound by their Rules of Professional Conduct to charge a reasonable fee. What a "reasonable" fee is depends on a variety of factors. While the rule varies somewhat from state to state, a summarized rule would provide as follows:

- The amount of the fee in proportion to the value of the services performed.

- The relative sophistication of the lawyer and the client.

- The novelty and difficulty of the questions

involved and the skill required to perform the legal service properly.

◆ The likelihood, if apparent to the client, that the acceptance of the particular employment will preclude other employment by the attorney.

◆ The amount involved and the results obtained.

◆ The time limitations imposed by the client or by the circumstances.

◆ The nature and length of the professional relationship with the client.

◆ The experience, reputation, and ability of the attorney or attorneys performing the services.

◆ Whether the fee is fixed or contingent.

◆ The time and labor required.

◆ The informed consent of the client to the fee.

Types of Compensation

Hourly-rate cases are those in which the attorney or paraprofessional/paralegal charges you for each hour or fraction thereof (one-tenth or one-quarter, generally) spent on your case. For instance, a six-minute phone conversation at two hundred dollars per hour is one-tenth of an hour, or twenty dollars.

Rates will generally vary between partners, associates, and paralegals with the more trained and experienced professionals commanding higher rates. Certain legal specialists, such as tax attorneys, patent attorneys, etc., may also command higher than average fees.

The location of the firm will affect rates since firms in fancy office buildings will probably have higher rent, and legal practitioners in major metropolitan areas face higher personnel costs and higher overhead than rural or suburban practitioners. You will generally find higher rates on the East Coast than the West, although San Francisco and Los Angeles may belie that trend. Midwest metropolitan areas will generally have rates comparable to East Coast cities.

The overhead of the firm will also place pressure on fee structures. Location, as earlier indicated, is only one factor in a firm's overhead. To which consumer or business demographic is the firm marketing its services? Firms which market to Fortune 1000 companies will tend to have more elaborate, corporate styled offices, whereas consumer-oriented firms tend to be less ostentatious.

What is the cost of their talent? Firms that seek to hire the best and brightest will also tend to pay top dollar to recruit and retain associates on a partnership track.

What is the staffing ratio? While two lawyers per support staff has been the norm, the growth of larger administrative, financial, and marketing support groups for firms has warped that ratio. In addition, if partners tend to monopolize staff, the ratio gets closer to one to one. Higher staffing costs will ultimately be passed down to the client.

An attorney found himself standing before the Pearly Gates. He went up to St. Peter and complained, "St. Peter, you have made a mistake. I am only thirty-six years old, and I am too young to die from natural causes."

St. Peter looked down on the attorney from his perch on high and frowned. "We couldn't have made a mistake. We added up your time sheets, and you should be eighty-eight years old."

The exponential growth in law firms' overhead also creates enormous pressure on attorneys to produce high-dollar billing sheets, whether they work in large or small firms. Unfortunately, this drive to be more business-like has also diminished some of the higher-calling aspects of the profession.

One of the more pernicious examples of the foregoing pressure is the unfortunate trend towards padding the attorney's time charges. This padding can sometimes occur at the administrative level by surcharging the attorney's time at the data-entry level, but more commonly, it occurs at the attorney's desk. An item that takes six minutes is billed at twelve or eighteen minutes. A project that takes thirty minutes is billed at an hour.

There are firms that require and/or reward their partners and associates for billing out 2,200 to 2,300 hours per year, or more. The pressures to meet these goals can be subtle, but no one in the legal trenches is dumb enough to believe the contrary rhetoric or lip service for accurate billing. All he or she has to do is watch who gets promoted or rewarded. Hopefully, your attorney interview process revealed these practices before your case progressed too far.

Now think about that goal for a minute. If a person works fifty out of fifty-two weeks a year, that goal would be achieved by working merely forty-four billable hours a week, or about nine hours a day for five days. The first obvious problem arises when you realize that with holidays, etc. most people do not work fifty weeks a year. It is probably closer to forty-eight weeks with four weeks given over to vacations and holidays. Now our weekly time allotment goes to approximately forty-six billable hours per week. Why, lots of people work more than forty-six hours per week, right?

The difference is that most people are not billing you $250 to $400 per hour while they put in their forty-six hours per week. The difference is those forty-six hours are not the time simply spent between nine a.m. and six p.m., Monday through Friday, but supposedly time spent researching the law, drafting pleadings or contract, performing legal analysis, negotiating for a client, or court appearances. It is "billable time."

To achieve nine hours of billable time in a nine-a.m.-to-six-p.m. day would require foregoing lunch, coffee breaks, chats with co-workers, calls from friends, family, or spouse, travel time, dead ends, wasted efforts, or any other interruption that was not pure, unadulterated billable time. In reality, to achieve nine hours of "billable" time in a day would generally take twelve or more hours of "work" time.

The emotional cost can be grueling. Even if you exerted twelve hours per day for five days a week, for a lawyer trying to be honest in his billings, can you imagine the grind such a day-in and day-out career would do to that person, his or her mental health, and the health of the attorney's family life? Can you imagine the lack of passion that attorney may bring to your case or lack of empathy for your cause? He or she may simply be too stressed out to give a damn about your case. Pay attention to the human elements in your team relationship with your attorney. Just as such emotional elements are important to you, so too can they be an important component to the attorney.

The other problem which arises with worshipping the hourly rate is lawyers lose sight of whether they are providing value to their clients. It may come as a surprise to some people that charging by the hour is a recent trend in the legal profession. We use "recent" in the context of a profession that still cites cases that are three hundred years old. Slightly more than forty-five years ago, many lawyers used standard fee tables issued by their local bar associations, contingent or fixed fees, or some approximation of the effort expended. Standard fee tables were thrown out in the late 1960s on anti-trust grounds.

Then studies appeared that showed firms that billed on a systematic, hourly-rate basis made more money than their contemporaries that "weighed" the file and charged what they thought was a fair approximation of a reasonable fee. Forty-five years later, the hourly rate practice is essentially enshrined in the profession as the Holy Grail of client billing.

There are movements to change billing practices to the concept of "value billing," which attempts to seek a dialogue with the client over expectations and the client's view of the value of the resolution of the dispute or matter. The attorney and client then negotiate what a fair and reasonable fee would be, based upon the value brought to the transaction by the attorney's activities.

While many people have experimented with this concept, it does not appear to have caught on, primarily because most clients have not been able to cogently describe the value of a dispute as opposed to some transaction, such as buying and selling. Attorneys, on the other hand, loathe to be held too accountable for results of a case, which is still largely out of their exclusive control.

Black Holes for Hourly Rate Clients

Be alert to the following common black holes for clients and their money.

Double Team

Just like Mary and her lamb, everywhere the partner or senior associate goes, so goes one or more junior associates. This is the proverbial double and triple teaming. It is often justified that the associate is there in some important collaborative function, when in reality they are generally highly paid note-takers or "bag carriers."

Many times the double and triple teaming is the law-firm equivalent of a training program, similar to a training physician taking all the interns on medical rounds. When you start seeing multiple entries on the same day for the same event, ask pointed questions about the purpose of multiple attorneys and insist such double teaming stop unless your attorney convinces you of its need. This overstaffing problem can also be carried over into paralegals.

Endless Meetings

Internal status meetings can occur where everybody with a remote interest in your case is in attendance and bills you accordingly. There are three problems with getting billed for these status meetings. First, it would have been cheaper for a quick status memo to be circulated by email or print memo. Second, why does everyone have to be there for your case? Who has the information to be shared, and who is making the decision? Third, if the status of your case was discussed in two minutes, you can count on your bill reflecting .2 of an hour times the number of personnel in the room.

Unfortunately, two minutes of actual time equates to .033 of an hour. When you are dealing with everyone's billable rate, this difference between standard billing units and actual time begins to add up. Question whether the firm has invested in more efficient means of communication. Challenge standard billing units when used by multiple time keepers.

Endless meetings can also occur by emails. Attorneys and staff can endlessly email one another questions, research, and answers. If you are going to be billed for emails, then insist any billable email be copied simultaneously to you. Read the emails, and if they begin to become repetitious, ask what is the value of such an exchange.

File Reviews

A file review can be legitimate or simply a time filler. What was the purpose of the review? What was the outcome of the review?

No Stone Left Unturned

Researching the law can be an incredibly time-intensive process, even with the most industrious and honest of lawyers. Sifting through cases, statutes, regulations, and legislative history to find the right historical cases could take days.

However, legal research has radically changed with the breadth and depth of legal information on the Internet and in fee-based websites, e.g., Lexis-Nexis or Westlaw sites.

Simple legal research can be done in a matter of minutes, and tougher questions may take several hours, but if days are charged just for research, ask about it. When you start seeing legal research popping up on your bills, find out the target of the research.

If you start to suspect your attorneys are turning over every stone, find out why that depth and breadth of research is required for the issues involved. Are your opponents making a motion that requires such research? Has any attempt been made to resolve disputes over legal issues with agreements between the various parties? If not, why not? Research can often be another training ground for associates and another way to increase billable hours. Stay alert. Push back if their answers seem too glib or dismissive.

Churning

Churning is a term familiar to investors and their stockbrokers, but it is a process equally applicable to lawyers. Lawyers churn, for instance, when they take overly aggressive positions and then enforce that position with motions that do little to advance the core issues of the case and only add expense to the client.

If your attorneys are making a lot of motions and you do not understand the point of such motions, you need to insist on an explanation. If you are not convinced, get the attorneys to adopt a more reasonable posture. Rambo tactics rarely work in the long term and only cost you money. Once again, keeping a firm eye on the cost-benefit equation will help you control costs.

Churning also includes situations where work is duplicated or recycled. If the firm completed the research and brief on almost identical issues in another case and then charges the second client the same amount of money, as if they originated the research for the second client, the firm is recycling work. While firms should not be punished for efficient use of past research, there should be some discount to the second client for the time actually involved or some limited surcharge for the value of the work provided.

Needless reviews can consume excessive time and create duplicate billing. If an associate reviews a pleading, for instance, and then a partner reviews it for more than a quick quality assurance, then why didn't the partner do the review in the first place? If a second- or third-draft review occurs, what changed from the prior draft that justifies the time spent in the review?

We Admit No Fact before Its Time

Many litigants believe that failing to admit facts which they recognize as true will only make the case harder for their opponents. They're absolutely right. Unfortunately, it will also add immeasurable amounts of billing charges to your account as your attorneys wrangle with opposing counsel over correctly alleged facts. Making life difficult for the opposing party is not only contrary to the rules of civil procedure but also only adds needless expense to your bottom line.

Discover the World

In litigation, "discovery" consists of written questions (interrogatories), requests for production of documents and things, requests for admission of facts, and various types of depositions.

In any case, there are witnesses and documents that are critical to a determination of liability or damages. These witnesses need to be questioned (deposed) and the documents obtained (request for production).

However, there are also peripheral witnesses and documents, which may or may not need to be questioned or produced, particularly if the cost of such deposition or production may outweigh the evidentiary value of the witness or document. These low-priority witnesses and document productions can consume large quantities of your funds with little tangible impact on your case.

Discovery can not only consume time but also increase your costs. If your attorneys start traveling the country, taking depositions, you will be paying their travel, lodging, and food per diems for these junkets. Expert witnesses will charge for the time they spend preparing for the depositions and attending the depositions. It costs money to have any deposition transcribed and copied.

First, have your attorneys prepare a discovery plan and justify the cost-benefit of each witness and set of documents. Otherwise, it would be cheaper to see the world by enlisting in the U.S. Navy.

Second, evaluate whether teleconference technology will allow depositions of far-flung witnesses to occur with your attorneys staying at home. There is also emerging Internet technology with specially equipped court reporters, which allows participants to stay at their desks and participate in real time in the depositions both visually and with two-way audio.

Other Discovery Abuses

Deposition digests used to be a fairly important tool in pre-computer days because it was important to know where key questions and answers were located. Clients may have wanted summaries of the deposition of certain witnesses. However, in today's world, court reporters can provide deposition transcripts that have already been indexed or in searchable formats so all questions, answers, and even words can be retrieved electronically. For example, www.reallegal.com provides a free download of its reader so you can view electronic transcripts. Some of the software to review depositions electronically can be downloaded for free. Ask your attorneys to request any depositions to be available in electronic formats you can access.

Computer software exists to analyze and scan depositions for the purpose of highlighting pertinent portions for trial purposes. Be wary of large amounts of time being spent on deposition summaries absent your specific request. Ask the firm to explain their use of technology in this regard and why it was not employed in your case.

Attorneys can spend large amounts of time creating and drafting interrogatory questions for your case. However, just how effective are these interrogatories in securing information? Probably not very effective at all. In some jurisdictions and in federal courts, there are limits on the number of interrogatories allowed. These limitations arose in recognition that interrogatories can become so detailed and overreaching that their practical utility becomes nil.

A common scenario is that a complicated and burdensome interrogatory is objected to by the opposing counsel or the answer is incomplete. Your attorney communicates with opposing counsel and argues over the legitimacy of the question's scope or relevance. Your attorney may file a motion to compel. Opposing counsel resists your motion and files briefs and affidavits to contest it.

Both attorneys end up spending hours in the courthouse, waiting to argue their motions. The results of such arguments are generally mixed, and the amount of information retrieved can continue to be stalled on other grounds. Meanwhile, the opposing counsel puts together their own burdensome interrogatories, and the entire process is repeated.

In the end, most of the interrogatories retrieve incomplete answers, and you foot the bill. Interrogatories serve a purpose in obtaining basic information about parties, witnesses, and available custodians of documents, but beyond these straightforward requests, the utility of interrogatories begins to drop precipitously. Discuss the types of interrogatories intended to be used in the attorney's discovery plan, and in this case, apply the KISS principle.

Another problem arises when your attorney sends a *subpoena duces tecum* for the production of documents as part of a notice of deposition, instead of using the standard request for production of documents, which requires thirty days prior notice. Predictably, the opposing counsel objects to this attempt to bypass the civil rules regarding discovery, and a flurry of motions, briefs, and hearings ensues. Who loses? Both clients.

I'm a Traveling Man

Travel time is a troublesome issue. Obviously, if an attorney is pulled out of the office, he or she experiences an opportunity cost in traveling for the client. On the other hand, travel outside of business hours is an inconvenience, but it is unlikely the attorney would have been working. Also, travel time is rarely spent in the same intellectual level of engagement as general work time, so why is the client being charged full hourly rates?

What if the attorney does work for another client? What if the trip is necessitated by two or more client matters and the attorney is simply being efficient in pooling his travel? Who pays for the time and costs in these scenarios? The client should question travel time policies up front and negotiate lower fees for work-hours travel and substantially reduced or non-existent charges for off-hours travel.

Who's Sally?

Staff turnover is a problem for both the client and the firm. Loss of continuity can be traumatic in a case of any complexity. All of a sudden, a complete stranger is on the phone or handling inquiries. Time is spent by the newcomer to get up to speed. Who pays for the transition? The firm should absorb the cost. Why?

Because it was their personnel that departed and their chosen personnel that took the departing employee's place.

The client had little to no input on the underlying reasons for the departure or for the choice of replacement. The expense of new personnel getting up to speed should be the responsibility of the firm, not the client. Pay attention if the personnel change leads to charges for file review.

Billable vs. Clerical Work

An awareness of the difference between attorney work and clerical work is important. If an attorney sits down at a computer and drafts documents, that is appropriate attorney time since dictating and revising the document in the traditional work pattern would consume a similar amount of time. Recycling forms is another related issue which we touched upon earlier in this chapter.

However, what if the attorney then spends time to copy the pleadings, organize them for service and processing, and ensures they are sent off to the legal messenger? The latter tasks are clerical in nature and are not worth the hourly rate of a highly compensated attorney. When you retain a firm, ask for clarification of the billing practices relative to clearly distinguishing clerical from professional work.

Some attorneys charge for word processing time spent by their secretaries. First, examine the engagement letter to discover if this type of billing is appropriate. Second, if every overhead item is being charged to the client, what is justification for the rate of the attorney, which traditionally was supposed to incorporate overhead items?

So What Is a Poor Client to Do?

Almost unbelievably, we recommend that clients do not get fixated on the hourly rate, but focus on the total cost to get the job done. For instance, a senior partner may be able to complete a task based on experience and connections in an hour at $350 per hour. A younger associate at $200 per hour may take three hours to complete the same project. Focusing on the hourly rate instead of the bottom line would be penny-wise and pound-foolish. But how do you get data to make the foregoing comparisons?

In any type of case, ask the attorney to provide you with some estimates of the fees and costs associated with the type of case based upon past experience. While a pinpoint estimate is impossible, there should be some range of fees and costs, which an experienced attorney can provide, with a description of the variables that may skew the estimate. Make it clear you expect the cost of the project to follow the estimate no matter who works on the project.

Ask for a budget estimate for the case if the complexity or issues justify that investment of time, with a breakdown of each component part of the case. For a litigation case, these categories may be (1) pre-litigation investigation and research, (2) preparation of complaint and filing, (3) plaintiff's discovery, (4) defendant's discovery, (5) pre-trial motions, (6) pre-trial preparation, (7) trial, (8) post-trial work.

A transaction matter may have budget lines for (1) due diligence, (2) negotiation, (3) drafting of documents, (4) closing of transaction, and (5) follow-up and recording, if any. Obviously, each type of case may have variables.

In addition, you need to ask the attorney for an estimate of costs for expert witnesses, trial exhibits, etc. See Appendix F for a sample litigation plan. This type of activity is more common in larger cases, but requesting such a budget would be a good exercise for the attorney to think through what is exactly needed in the case's development and provide you some estimates of time and costs.

Make sure the attorney will provide you with a detailed breakdown of time and costs in his or her billing. If you cannot ascertain what is being done, then the billings are not sufficiently detailed.

Review the billings and question what appears to be excessive time for the work or product produced. Challenge charges for time that are clearly in excess of the time spent. For instance, some firms charge in fifteen-minute intervals. Most firms charge for tenths of an hour, but even that six minutes can be excessive for a quick two-minute phone call. Most billing software can handle billing units as low as .01, but we recommend insisting on billing units of a minimum of .03 or three-minute intervals.

A quarter-hour charge for a two-minute phone call represents a charge 7.5 times greater than the accurate billing. Insist on accurate time billing and pay attention to the time you spend with the attorney by using your own diary and comparing it to your billing.

Negotiating Fees with Attorneys

It may surprise people to realize that you can negotiate fees with lawyers in advance of retaining them to handle a case. Now, this fact is not universal, but if done with some diplomacy and intelligence, most attorneys are willing at least to discuss the prospect of special fee arrangements in terms of hourly rates, percentages on contingent-fee cases, or the result achieved.

Your ability to negotiate a lower hourly rate will be hampered by your lack of bargaining clout unless you bring a great deal of business to the firm or your case is desirable to the attorney. However, do not be afraid to discuss hourly rates or contingent-fee percentages.

Pay your bill on time. Whatever deal you make, comply with it, or your good will with your attorney (e.g., encouraging him or her to put in the extra effort, etc.) will evaporate.

However, negotiating fees should not be limited simply to an hourly rate or percentage, but a more comprehensive and potentially creative approach to how your money is going to be spent. Even if we are talking about a contingent fee case, there are out-of-pocket expenses that mount up, which are taken out of your recovery.

The first rule you must understand is that lawyers have certain ethical restrictions with respect to handling the finances of a case. For instance, in the personal injury arena, in many states, lawyers may advance costs for a client, but the client must remain liable ultimately for those costs.

Asking an attorney ultimately to absorb these costs is asking the attorney to engage in unethical conduct under most state bar codes and probably will not create a friendly atmosphere with your intended attorney. Check with your bar association to determine if your state allows an attorney to absorb the litigation costs in a contingency-fee case.

Your Ethical Attorney

Accordingly, asking an attorney to do something unethical in order to save money is a tactic that might come back to haunt you or bite you back. If you choose an unethical attorney to save money in the short term, you might lose more in the long run. If an attorney will lie for you, then the attorney will lie to you.

Assuming ethical rules are being obeyed, the attorney is still in business to cover his or her overhead and make enough money to meet his or her own financial goals. Behind every negotiation over compensation is the business motivation to (1) obtain new cases/clients or increase the quality of cases being handled by the firm and (2) make more money than it costs to provide the service. There are some basic concepts in this dance of negotiation.

Contingent Fee

The most common billing format used in collection or personal injury cases is the contingent fee. Contingent fee cases are those wherein the attorney agrees to spend the time necessary to bring your claim to completion, either by settlement or litigation, for a percentage of your claim, plus out-of-pocket costs.

The fee is contingent because, absent recovery of some amount, there is no fee. One should always remember that in most states, costs are not contingent and are owed notwithstanding the outcome. Approximately eleven states allow the attorney to absorb the costs in hardship cases; but most states require the client to be ultimately responsible.

However, since the time spent by the attorney is by far the largest investment in a case, the contingent fee removes most of the downside risk of a legal representative's expense from the client.

The key to understanding your bottom line in negotiating a contingent fee is to understand that an attorney's time commitment to a case is very much like climbing up one small hill, going down into the valley, and climbing up another higher hill to the summit. Initially, pulling together a case takes a certain amount of concentrated time: the small hill. After that initial effort, however, there is a varying period of time where the case commitment may hit a lull in activity due to court delays, other deadlines, or scheduling issues: the valley.

However, once discovery processes start, and true trial preparation begins, then the time and expense start to climb rather precipitously out of the valley. Because of this reality, some law firms charge a higher percentage contingent fee when litigation or trial commences or upon an appeal. Other law firms simply charge a flat percentage fee no matter to what stage of the process they pursue the matter.

Your Fee Arrangement

Depending upon the nature and risks of your case, one or another of these methods may be a fair tradeoff; however, you are still in the driver's seat in determining a fee arrangement with which you are comfortable.

When negotiating over a contingent fee, pay attention to the following principles:

1. If the attorney refuses to discuss any adjustments in her or his fee, however politely he or she refuses, just as politely indicate that some accommodation is expected.

2. Negotiate one or more of the following concessions:

    a) The contingent fee only applies to the amount in excess of the insurance company's last written offer to you prior to retaining the attorney or some predetermined amount you negotiate as your bottom-line recovery. Keep in mind economic reality; otherwise, the attorney will refuse your case if at the outset he or she cannot make any money representing you.

b) Reduce the overall percentage initially and then increase as the time expenditure in the case increases. By way of example, the fee structure might be 20 percent until litigation is commenced, 25 percent when a summons and complaint are filed, 33 percent if the case actually goes to trial, and 40 percent if there is a successful appeal and recovery. These are only examples, and each case may vary.

c) Reduce the percentage fee when the recovery exceeds certain levels; for instance, if the recovery exceeds one hundred thousand dollars, then the fee percentage applied to every dollar above one hundred thousand dollars is 10 percent. The rationale is that many times it doesn't take any more time to process a hundred-thousand-dollar case than a twenty-five-thousand-dollar case.

d) Don't give away your money. Have out-of-pocket legal costs taken off the top of the recovery before computation of the fee. ("Costs" do not include your economic damages, like medical expenses or wage loss.)

e) Get the attorney to agree that no contingent fee will apply to your standard property damage recovery for automobile repair or total loss. Why? There is not enough equity in the property damage settlements to cover a contingent fee since they rarely cover loans. Taking a contingent fee for property damage only rubs salt in the wound.

There are also services available which will negotiate your property damage claim for flat fees.

f) Obtain an agreement from the attorney that his or her contingent fee will not exceed your net recovery. In this concession, the attorney would compute his or her normal fee, and if higher than the net recovery, then transfer dollars to the client's net recovery until the client recovery and attorney fee are equal.

3. Get any agreement regarding fees in writing to avoid misunderstandings. Most states require such agreements. If your attorney objects to this requirement, find another attorney. (See Appendix B for a suggested format.)

4. Ask the attorney for a cost budget or estimate, and make sure that the attorney must seek your consent before incurring more than an agreed-upon threshold amount. However, remember that the attorney has little or no control over the charges made by healthcare professionals or expert witnesses in compiling documentation and preparing for a trial.

While using a contingent fee may seem the answer to the client's concerns over the cost of representation, remember that the attorney is gauging the amount of time he or she may have to spend on the case versus the likely economic result. For example, in an anticipated $25,000 case, do not expect the attorney to knowingly or willingly expend $10,000 in time (by way of example) when, under a one-third-contingent fee, the attorney would only receive $8,300 from a $25,000 settlement.

The client needs to discuss with the attorney what work needs to be done to properly prepare the case and then monitor the attorney's performance to make sure the work is done. Otherwise, if an attorney begins to believe the investment of time will exceed the fee, then the attorney may be tempted to cut corners or try to convince the client to settle the case quickly to reduce future time expenditures. This is a delicate ethical situation for the attorney who is expected to place the client's interest in front of the attorney's economic well-being.

It must also be differentiated from the situation where the attorney sincerely believes the case has reached its highest settlement value, and further work will not increase the offers. At such a juncture, the attorney will need to apprise the client of the respective costs and benefits of settling or proceeding to trial with all its uncertainties and costs. Trust in your attorney's motivation is an essential component to understanding the difference in these scenarios. The best way to avoid this ethical dilemma is to have the discussion regarding settlement scenarios at the commencement of the case, instead of down the road when settlement advice may be suspect.

Delegation to Paralegals

Most attorneys use paralegals to handle many of the day-to-day requirements of the case, so do not be surprised by this delegation. It allows the attorney to take cases that would not make economic sense without such less expensive personnel.

By the same token, if the attorney will be using paralegal staff, you should ask about their qualifications, experience, and workload, as well to ensure your case does not become a backwater case because of either paralegal inexperience or overload.

Flat Fee

Flat fee agreements are simply what they purport to be, a flat fee in exchange for defined services. Flat fee agreements are common in misdemeanor criminal cases, DWI/DUI cases, or cases which have highly predictable time expenditures, such as estate planning, closing transactions, and probate. They do not constitute the majority of fee structures, although with the aforementioned professional movement towards value billing, flat fee types of agreements, in whole or in part, may soon appear in a greater variety of cases.

By way of example, one might agree with an insurance company to arbitrate a case. Then you can negotiate with an attorney to handle only the arbitration process for some fixed fee plus costs. You will discover a lot of resistance to flat fees from civil (as opposed to criminal) trial attorneys because they are not common, and many attorneys have never been requested to provide precisely defined services for flat fees.

Be Concerned about Competence, Not Brilliance

While there are potentially thorny legal problems that can arise in a legal case, where a brilliant attorney may be required, the vast majority of legal matters require only a well-informed competence in the following areas:

1. Relatively simple legal issues arising in common consumer and business cases.

2. An attention to detail in generating supporting documentation.

3. A calm and focused negotiating ability in the face of potentially hostile or outwardly disinterested negotiators or adverse attorneys.

4. An appreciation for the realistic strengths, weaknesses, and value of your case versus the subjective
   strength and value of your injuries as perceived by
   you and your Aunt Tilly who received an obscene
   amount of money twenty years ago for a stubbed toe.

None of these areas is beyond the ken of the average consumer,
although prudence dictates that you rely upon attorneys more
often than not for legal issues. In short, you do not need the
best and the brightest with their predictable unwillingness to
negotiate or high cost to assist you.

Pay Attention to Your Bottom Line

In a contract case, there could be a range of damage scenarios,
depending upon the complexity of the contractual relationship
and duration. However, even in a simple damage case, there must
be an assessment of the liability issues, and bottom-line issues.
If you do not have a mechanism to retrieve attorney's fees, then
the cost of recovery comes out of your ultimate recovery.

If there is a chance for the cost of recovery to exceed your claim,
then prudence would dictate a more conciliatory approach to
the dispute. If there are likely to be counterclaims assessed back
against you, then the likelihood of their success needs to be
factored into your decision to proceed with litigation.

A personal injury case presents potentially even more daunting
challenges. Assuming for the sake of argument that a personal
injury claim has a value capable of objective determination,
you must view the process of achieving that economic goal as
one associated with certain costs of doing business. Even if you
never consult an attorney, there will be costs associated with
obtaining records, reports, etc., and there is still the opportunity
cost of your own time.

A Personal Injury Case Study

In a personal injury claim, your bottom line is determined as follows:

Gross settlement Value	$50,000
LESS Claim Costs	($1,000)
LESS Unpaid Health Costs	($5,000)
LESS Subrogation	($4,000)
LESS Attorney's Fees	($16,000)
TOTAL RECOVERY (BOTTOM LINE)	$24,000

In a pre-litigation context, your claim costs will vary somewhat, depending on the number of providers you have utilized and the need for narrative reports versus chart notes and bills. When you use an attorney, the attorney is charged for all of these items and passes those costs on to your account.

If you are representing yourself, many times health-care providers can be persuaded to give you copies of their records and bills at no or minimal cost (excluding narrative reports). However, for the sake of this illustration, pre-litigation costs average $500-$1,000. Once litigation commences, these costs start to escalate sharply.

Your Costs During Litigation

The combination of your contractual obligation to reimburse your own carriers for their payments for medical care and wage loss (subrogation) and the unpaid balance remaining at time of settlement often represents the single largest component of your recovery, sometimes even eclipsing your attorney's fees, if any.

Let us assume that you and the adjuster have independently determined that your claim is worth $50,000. (You can rest assured that adjusters will not disclose their real valuation to you, nor will they offer such sum to you if they can avoid it.)

The insurance company's first offer to you is $5,000. We are not going to concern ourselves in this example with reimbursement of medical costs or subrogation interests. Nor are we going to complicate this example with recovery risk assessments, though recovery risk does play a role in any value analysis.

Marginal cost in a personal injury setting is the cost required to move the insurance company, willingly or unwillingly (through arbitration or litigation), from the existing offer ($5,000) to the perceived value ($50,000).

Excluding attorney's fees for a moment, costs include such items as filing fees, costs for medical reports and records, expert witness fees for depositions and trial appearances, and discovery costs in the nature of transcription costs and document reproduction. From the perspective of a consumer, the attorney's fees you incur, by either hourly rate or contingent-fee percentage, are a cost associated with moving forward with a claim.

Assume the non-fee cost of moving the insurance company to a settlement value of $50,000 is $1,000. Assume further your attorney was charging you one-third of the gross amount. If you were able to obtain our hypothetical $50,000, your net recovery would be $24,000 versus doing nothing more and taking $5,000. The enhancement of your bottom line would mitigate in favor of spending the costs and moving forward.

However, the closer you reach the $24,000 on your own, and taking into account the recovery risk factor, cost of litigation, and attorney's fees, you might wish to settle for much less than the hypothetical claim value of $50,000 rather than hiring an attorney, taking more time to settle or resolve the claim in the hope of achieving a gross settlement of $50,000. In the foregoing scenario, you may be able to reach a settlement that, while less than the hypothetical case value, is still close to your hypothetical best-case bottom line.

Checklist and Reminders

☑ Compensation arrangements need to be mutually beneficial, or the relationship will suffer.

☑ Attorneys are ethically required to charge reasonable fees as determined by the eight-point list in this chapter. Do not be intimidated by hourly rates quotes without reference to those factors.

☑ Negotiating fees with attorneys is more than simply reducing rates, but with some creativity, your fees can be aligned with results and the attorney's amount of effort.

☑ Different compensation structures can be applied to different types of cases, and even combined in hybrid arrangements to fit your mutual financial needs and abilities.

☑ Use a cost-benefit analysis about how time and expense are expended for your case, and monitor the attorney to ensure these cost-benefit objectives are met.

CHAPTER NINE
PREPAID LEGAL PLANS

GOALS

1. Understand prepaid legal plans
2. Explore the pros and cons of membership

Prepaid Legal—To Buy or Not to Buy?

There are dozens of legal service plans across the country, some available on a national level and others locally or regionally.

Legal service plans are available with a variety of benefits but generally provide legal advice and consultation by telephone. Most plans will also provide some document reviews, simple wills, forms, and discount fees from panel attorneys. Benefits will also vary from state to state, depending on regulatory requirements or restrictions.

Prepaid Legal Services, Inc., for instance, has a variety of plans, which provide review of simple legal documents, preparation of a simple will, traffic ticket defense, discount services, and drafting of letters or phone calls addressed to adverse parties designed to resolve conflicts early. Some plans offer more comprehensive coverage for trials, marital problems, bankruptcy, real estate matters, and similar legal issues.

Most legal plans are not insurance. They do not reimburse you or pay your attorney for services rendered. There are very few such legal insurance plans available, and generally they offer their plans to employers and employer groups.

You should also pay attention to whether the plan retains its panel attorneys on the basis of discount fees for you or whether the attorneys work for a discounted fee payable by the legal service plan.

Most legal service plans charge for individual or family benefits in a range of nine dollars to twenty-five dollars per month, as of the date of this printing, chargeable to your credit card or banking account. Business legal service plans are also available from some plans and in some states for higher rates. The monthly cost for such business plans can range from fifty to one hundred dollars per month, or higher in some cases.

Some employers may also provide legal service plans as an employee benefit. As of mid-1995, there were more than eighteen million Americans enrolled in legal service plans, according to the American Prepaid Legal Services Institute. For more information, you can access their website at www.aplsi.org.

One program we have previously mentioned, which is worth more than a cursory look, is Pre-Paid Legal Services, Inc. (www.prepaidlegal.com) with headquarters in Oklahoma. Pre-Paid Legal Services promotes telephone access, discount fees, and individual, professional, and small-business plans. For an individual family plan, for a relatively inexpensive fee per month, you have unlimited access during business hours to attorneys for a myriad of questions and document reviews. The company has been in the business for years and has coverage in most states and Canada.

Prepaid legal plans are an ideal method of handling your legal informational needs while negotiating a simple problem/matter on your own. Check with your state's insurance commissioner to see what other legal care plans are registered to do business in your state.

A partial listing of legal service plans is also available at www. aplsi.org/legal_plans.

CHAPTER TEN

UNDERSTANDING THE AMERICAN JUSTICE SYSTEM

Law Primer

In order to understand discussions about lawyers, we must provide a primer on the organization of the law and some of its theoretical or philosophical divisions.

First, without debating the moral or natural law underpinning any legal system, the hierarchy of the law in the United States flows first from the U.S. Constitution, then to the three branches of government, executive, legislative (Congress), and judicial. The legislative branch creates law through the passage of statutes, which are then codified into the United States Code.

The federal executive branch, through its agencies, is subject to legislative mandates and creates regulations to clarify and enforce such statutes. Since the authority and budgets of agencies depend upon Congressional approval and delegation, regulations must be based upon statutory authority and cannot exceed the scope of statutory delegation.

Checks and Balances

The fiscal and regulatory interplay between the executive branch's agencies and the Congress is part of the constitutional checks and balances our Constitution builds into the system. A comprehensive treatment of this subject is well beyond the scope of this field guide but is a fascinating topic for future study.

Completing the triangle is the judicial branch, which can interpret the application of statutes and regulations to specific factual disputes, rule such statutes as unconstitutional or regulations as outside the parameters of Congressional delegation, or in the absence of either statute or regulation, create rights and duties as the judicial interpretation of the transcendent common law.

States' Rights

Second, the governmental structure of every state in the Union, with the exception of Nebraska with its unicameral legislature, is basically a rough carbon copy of the federal system. Each state's constitution is authorized as a byproduct of either participation in the Constitutional Convention or by virtue of a Congressional enabling act. Each state has its executive, legislative, and judicial branches, with the interplay of statutes, regulations, and case law. However, each state's laws and regulations have their substantive and procedural differences.

Third, the interplay between federal and state law can become complicated. For our purposes, in those areas where federal law has jurisdiction by virtue of the commerce clause or similar national purpose, state law is subservient. State law may co-exist with federal laws and may be more strict than federal law but may not dilute or diminish the requirements of federal law.

Federal Pre-emption

The exception to this latter rule is the concept of federal pre-emption, in which the Congress indicates that ONLY federal law applies and any other state attempt to regulate the pre-empted area is void. A good example of this pre-emption exists where the provisions of ERISA (Employee Retirement Income Security Act), when applicable to the claim, have been interpreted to pre-empt certain state laws, which would tend to alter the rights and benefits available to beneficiaries under ERISA, such as insurance subrogation rights and limitations.

Criminal, Commercial, and Procedural Law

Fourth, yet another division of the law separates substantive law and procedural law. Substantive law constitutes the rules concerning rights and duties of people vs. people or people and property. Statutes defining criminal behavior would be an example of substantive law. The Uniform Commercial Code, adopted and revised in most states, provides substantive law on a variety of business and banking transactions.

By contrast, procedural law deals with rules regarding the dispute resolution process before judicial or administrative tribunals, and other governmental processes. Court rules governing how courts operate are procedural in nature.

Substantive law may be viewed as the "what" and procedural law as the "how." Though procedural law may be mistakenly considered less important than substantive provisions of the law, failing to abide by either category's dictates can impair or forfeit your claim. When it comes to dealing with your legal affairs, it is wise to ignore a generational adage and instead, "Sweat the small details."

Civil and Criminal Law

Fifth, the law is oftentimes separated into two great categories, civil law and criminal law. Personal injury, contract disputes, and property transactions are examples of the category of civil law. In civil cases, the parties must either resolve their disputes privately or resort to mediation, arbitration, or the court system.

Both civil law and criminal law deal with human behavior and the relationships between people and property. What distinguishes criminal from civil is a recognition that certain types of behavior are so threatening to society or to individual rights that the State must sanction the behavior by labeling the behavior as criminal conduct and impose state-mandated imprisonment or fine or both. In addition, what traditionally separated unlawful criminal acts from unlawful civil acts was the criminal intent of the perpetrator, the requisite *mens rea* (guilty mind).

Intent and Foreseeable Consequences

Today, in some classes of criminal conduct, that intent can be blurred somewhat by a concept that proposes we intend the foreseeable consequences of our actions. For instance, when you drink and drive, you may have absolutely no intent to crash your vehicle and injure other people. However, you are held to the knowledge that if you drink and drive the foreseeable consequence of that behavior may be a collision and injury. Hence, once you drink and then climb into the driver's seat, for criminal purposes, the results are intentional. In criminal cases, it is not left up to the aggrieved parties to punish, but that task is delegated to the prosecutorial arm of the governmental agency having jurisdiction.

The Mystery of Torts

A term often used by attorneys is the term "tort." A "tort" within a legal context, as compared to a "torte" in the baking context, is an unlawful civil infringement or invasion of a person's rights or property. What sometimes confuses people is the fact that a given behavior, for instance, striking someone in the face (battery), can be simultaneously a tort, or violation of civil law, and a violation of criminal law.

The two areas of conduct are NOT mutually exclusive. In addition, if you are charged with criminal assault and battery and sued for civil tort of assault and battery, the result you achieve in one forum, criminal court, does not preordain the result you might later receive in the civil court. The criminal and civil cases against O. J. Simpson are a good example of this dual application of civil and criminal remedies. Thus Mr. Simpson could be found not guilty of criminal charges, but guilty within a civil court context.

Beyond a Reasonable Doubt

The reason for the distinction is not only the varying definitional differences between the two allegations, the requirement of criminal intent for the crime and the absence of intent for the civil claim, but also the level of required evidence for the criminal charge to be sustained. Excluding administrative and traffic infraction charges, criminal charges must be proven beyond a reasonable doubt.

Preponderance of the Evidence

Civil claims only need be proven by the preponderance of the evidence. Everyone who ever watched *Perry Mason* or the late Henry Fonda's role in *Twelve Angry Men* understands "beyond a reasonable doubt." It means everyone on the jury, being reasonable men or women, do not doubt the evidence demonstrates the defendant is guilty as charged. It is not the absence of any doubt but the absence of reasonable doubt that allows the State to punish the accused.

"Preponderance of the evidence," by contrast, is simply a measure of proof that means more evidence suggests a fact is true than suggests the fact is false. Preponderance can literally mean 51 percent of the facts point to liability, while 49 percent of the facts point to non-liability. Assuming all facts are equal (and they are not in reality), then in this example, liability has been proven by the preponderance of the evidence. As implied, preponderance of the proof is not so mechanical as adding up factual points but has the lesser burden of proof as compared to reasonable doubt.

Court Hierarchy

The court system is constructed in a hierarchical fashion. Some form of initial trial court forms the base of the pyramid. In the state of Washington, by way of example, certain cities are allowed to have municipal courts that handle violations of city ordinances. Counties have limited jurisdiction courts, called district or justice courts, to handle state mandated misdemeanors and civil cases with damages under fifty thousand dollars. The number of justice courts for each county varies with the county's population and size.

Each county has its primary courts of record, called superior courts in Washington State, which have unlimited jurisdiction to hear all cases of a criminal or civil nature. The first level of appellate courts is entitled the court of appeals, and there are three such courts situated around the state. The highest state appellate court is called the Washington State Supreme Court.

Right to Appeal

As a general rule, persons involved in civil court disputes have the right to at least one appeal from the trial court, and thereafter, any further appeals are at the discretion of the higher appellate court. Every state has a slightly different structure and nomenclature for its courts, so the Washington State nomenclature is not universal across the United States. However, most states have the pyramid structure of lower trial courts and higher appellate courts.

Right and Duty

Before we leave this discussion of the justice system, let us explore one philosophical concept: For every right there is a corresponding duty. In short, rights do not exist in a social and legal vacuum, devoid of someone else's duties. In all too many ways, we have become a nation preoccupied with our rights and too undisciplined or self-centered to pay attention to duty.

Take a moment and dwell on this duality. Define any right, and if valid, all others in society must have a corresponding duty to respect it. If you have a right to do something, then society, through civil or criminal law, must be prepared to uphold that right and society's corresponding duty to allow the exercise of that behavior.

The next time you wish to speak about your rights, reverse the discourse and ask yourself if you wish to exercise the duty to let someone behave the exact same way to you without recrimination or recourse of any kind. If not, you might want to reexamine the basis for your assertion that your rights fit into the social fabric.

Dispute Resolution Structures

If parties fail to negotiate away their differences, then absent a walk-away option, they will undoubtedly be forced to choose one or more dispute-resolution mechanisms. Old-fashioned litigation—the court, judge, and jury in a protracted battle—is the best known. However, other options exist.

Mediation

In its simplest form, mediation is a more formal negotiation process, which is overseen by a trained facilitator, known as a mediator. The parties present their positions either in joint session or privately to the mediator. The mediator then engages the sides in a discussion of the pros and cons of their cases and tries to work the parties towards an acceptable settlement.

At its heart, mediation is purely voluntary, and there are no internal penalties for failing to compromise and settle a case or dispute. The mediator cannot impose a solution upon the parties. The mediator can only reason with the parties and try to persuade them to alter their positions into mutually acceptable postures.

Mediation can occur through the agreement of the parties, by court order, or by the imposition of the process by statute, notably in labor-management disputes. Mediations can be fairly low-key negotiations or occur around the classic dog-and-pony show presentation by either or both sides of their respective cases.

You may choose to bring an attorney with you to explain legal aspects of any client position or opposing party legal allegations, but you are the main focus of attention. You are much more involved in a mediation than you would be during the presentation of your case in arbitration or litigation.

Although not mediation in the strict sense, there are two other non-binding approaches to resolving a dispute.

Summary Jury Trial

What is sometimes referred to as a summary jury trial involves the attorneys presenting their respective cases in a summary fashion, without witnesses, before a jury of hired individuals and a judge. Once both sides have presented their case, the judge provides jury instructions to the jury panel, and they deliberate and present a decision. Such a decision is generally agreed in advance not to be binding. However, the jury is interviewed to develop their reasoning, and that information is available to both sides to aid in negotiating a resolution to their claims and dispute.

Mock Trial or Mini-trial

A mock trial or mini-trial can also be presented to a neutral facilitator and owners/executives of both parties. Once the presentation is completed, the neutral facilitator provides his or her decision, and then the owners/executives convene without their attorneys to resolve the dispute, if possible.

Arbitration

Unlike mediation, in arbitration the arbitrator will make a decision, and mechanisms exist to enforce that decision. Binding arbitration can be subject to appellate review under certain circumstances.

Arbitration can be imposed by contractual agreements, by post-dispute agreements of the parties, by statute, or by court. For instance, in the state of Washington, counties have the option of requiring monetary claims under specified dollar amounts of being diverted into mandatory arbitration, subject to a right of appeal to a *de novo* trial. (*"De novo"* means you retry the entire case.) If the appealing party fails to improve their position, then they must pay the post-arbitration attorney's fees of their opponent.

However, absent statute or contract, parties will not be able to take advantage of arbitration unless all parties agree to submit the dispute to this type of forum.

While arbitrations are more informal than court trials and the rules of evidence typically more relaxed, arbitrations still require the presentation of witnesses, documents, cross-examination, and oral argument. More likely than not, you will require attorneys to be part of your team to ensure a proper presentation is made.

Private Judging

Private judging is an alternative to formal litigation, and its advantages are faster scheduling of the evidentiary hearing, generally agreed-upon discovery, and binding result. The "judge" can be a retired judge agreeable to both parties, an attorney with pro tem experience, or an attorney with expertise in the issues being presented but who is otherwise neutral. While the cost of hiring such a judge will exceed the cost of using the civil court system, the savings in attorney fees and quicker resolution can often offset the expense.

Lawsuit

A lawsuit is started by delivering to the other party a paper called a COMPLAINT, which indicates he or she is being sued as a result of the dispute or claim. A complaint is accompanied by a SUMMONS, which indicates to the other party his or her obligation to respond. The party against which a lawsuit is brought is called a DEFENDANT or RESPONDENT. The party bringing the lawsuit is entitled PLAINTIFF or PETITIONER.

The defendant will generally retain his or her own attorney. Typically in the context of a personal injury claim, the insured defendant takes these papers to his or her insurance company, which delivers them to its lawyers. The insurance company's lawyers then deliver to plaintiff's legal counsel a NOTICE OF APPEARANCE and ultimately an ANSWER, in which they admit or deny the defendant's factual allegations about the dispute or claim.

Settlement

Even though a lawsuit may be started, settlement is always possible and should be explored as soon as possible in most cases. In personal injury cases, it is generally not advisable to seek settlement until the full extent of the injuries and response to treatment is understood.

One note about legal jargon. The word "pleadings" will be used extensively in any litigation because it encompasses the bulk of all paperwork generated in the case. The reference arises from the fact that parties seeking redress in medieval times would petition the King and make their "plea" for relief or redress. For example, there are courts of common pleas. Hence, when a modern-day litigant goes to court, he or she is still making a plea to the court for relief or redress, and the documentation is referred to as "pleadings."

Time and Expense

Of the above methods of dispute resolution, litigation can be the most time consuming and expensive. A standard claim will take fifteen to eighteen months from time of filing until trial in Seattle, Washington, and longer in other metropolitan areas. During that period of time, there will be discovery matters, motions, and other preparation conducted. It concludes with a trial in front of a judge and possibly a jury. It is the judge and/or jury under the guidance of the judge that decides whether you win or lose. The trial may take several days or weeks or months, depending upon the complexity of the case. While litigation is a last resort, sometimes there is simply no alternative.

Discovery

Once the lawsuit has been started, both sides have the right to obtain information by discovery deposition, interrogatories, request for production of documents, inspections, or when applicable, medical examination.

A discovery deposition is the testimony of some party or witness given under oath before a court reporter who takes down the testimony verbatim. This testimony can be used later to refresh recollections or stop a witness from changing his or her story or used at trial in place of an absent or deceased witness or party. Prior to a deposition, you should meet with your attorney to prepare yourself, or if the deposition is another person, to assist the attorney in understanding the relevance of the witness being deposed.

Interrogatories are written questions, which either attorney may submit and which have to be answered in writing, under oath, within thirty days of being received by mail.

A request for production of documents is just what it sounds like, a request to review documents, which the parties may use at trial. Attorneys are always looking for the smoking gun, which contradicts the other party's testimony. Whenever you are forwarded interrogatories or requests for production, it is very important that you immediately respond and provide the requested answers and documents. Procrastination will only generate motions to compel and sanctions.

Defense Medical Examinations

When bodily injury or mental health is an issue in the case, the defendant has a limited right to have you examined by a physician of his or her choice in accordance with court civil rules. Many times a defense medical exam is scheduled before litigation in the hope of expediting settlement. You should carefully read the material supplied in the appendices regarding attendance at a defense medical exam. The insurance company will pay for the cost of this examination, and a report will be given to the insurance company and your attorney about the defense doctor's findings and his or her opinions concerning your injuries.

Motions

A "motion" is a form of pleading that is addressed to the court and requests the court to take some action or compel action from one of the parties. Hence, a motion to dismiss is a request to terminate the case. A motion to compel discovery is asking the court to make another party answer the interrogatories or other discovery requests of the moving party.

A motion for summary judgment is raised when there are no legitimate issues of material fact, and the law grants the moving party the requested relief. Obviously, the basis for such a motion rarely exists in litigation since material facts are often at issue. However, you will see attorneys attempting to dismiss parts of a case with summary judgment motions. From the client's standpoint, the time consumed in these motions should be analyzed in advance, and unless there is a strong chance of success, motions for summary judgment are probably not worth the expense.

Trial

A trial occurs when the parties gather before a judge and present their witnesses and exhibits as evidence. In a bench trial, the judge is the fact-finder and makes the decision. In a jury trial, the jury is the fact-finder, and the judge provides the legal decisions.

The great majority of cases never are tried, even though lawsuits are started. Often, however, they are settled within just a few days before the trial date.

The following summarizes the parts of a trial, although some apply only to a trial by jury.

Jury Selection

The trial begins with jury selection. More accurately, jury selection is more aptly described as jury de-selection because you have the right to excuse a juror for cause, but otherwise you can get rid of jurors only through your pre-emptory challenges (generally three per side). Once one juror is excused, another juror from the panel of strangers is inserted, so you may end up with a worse person than you excused if you are not careful in your selection.

Opening Statements

After de-selecting a jury, the lawyers give an opening statement, which informs the jury about the case and what the lawyers intend to prove. Opening statements are not to contain argument, only a factual description of what happened.

Plaintiff's Case

Following opening statements, the plaintiff is entitled to present its documents and witnesses for its case in chief. Each witness will be examined by the plaintiff's counsel and then cross-examined by the defense.

Defense's Case

Once the plaintiff rests his or her case in chief, and assuming no motions are made by the defense, then the defense puts on its case in defense of the plaintiff's case and/or presents any counterclaims they may have filed. Once again, any witnesses are examined first by the defense and then cross-examined by the plaintiff.

Rebuttal

The defense rests, and the plaintiffs are entitled to present their rebuttal, although it is not common to do so unless something unexpected occurred in the defense's case or some point needs rehabilitation or reinforcement.

Jury Instructions

At this juncture, the attorneys will convene with the judge and decide on the instructions to be presented to the jury. This may take minutes or hours, depending on the case.

The jury instructions are read to the jury, and the lawyers proceed to make their closing arguments. Once closing arguments are concluded, the jurors are sequestered in the jury room and deliberate until they reach a decision or deadlock. Once they reach a decision, they return to the courtroom and the verdict is announced.

Following the verdict, additional pleadings are prepared and subsequently presented to the court for entry incorporating the jury's decision. Following the entry of such an order or judgment, the parties may agree with the decision or appeal.

Appeal

Both parties have a right to appeal to a higher court if they do not like the decision of the lower court. In the state of Washington, by way of example, from the lower district court, you have a right to appeal on the record to the county superior court. From the superior court, you have the right to appeal to the Washington State Court of Appeals.

Your right to appeal further to the Washington State Supreme Court is discretionary; the court may deny your petition for review. Stay of judgment and supersedeas bonds vary from state to state, and you should discuss these matters with your attorney. An appeal can be quite costly since generally you will have to provide a trial transcript and that can cost $750 or more per day of trial. In addition, the appellate process may take twelve months or longer to complete.

Checklist and Reminders

- ☑ Gain an understanding of the law pertinent to your case and the legal remedies available to you.

- ☑ Explore alternative mechanisms for resolution of disputes, such as mediation, arbitration, or rent a judge as a substitute for formal litigation.

- ☑ Assess the cost of prosecuting or defending litigation, and factor those costs and uncertainties into your settlement posture.

- ☑ Remember that preventive measure and a proactive relationships with your attorney are worth a ton of cure.

APPENDICES

APPENDIX A
ADDITIONAL READING

ATTORNEYS

Aronson, Robert H. H. *Professional Responsibility in a Nutshell.* West Publishing Company, 1991.

Foonberg, Jay. *Finding the Right Lawyer.* American Bar Association, 1995.

Powers, Dennis M. *Legal Expense Defense.* PSI Research/ The Oasis Press, 1995.

Ross, William G. *The Honest Hour.* Carolina Academic, 1996.

Seron, Carroll. *The Business of Practicing Law: The Work Lives of Solo and Small Firm Attorneys.* Temple University Press, 1996.

NEGOTIATION TACTICS and TECHNIQUES

Cohen, Herb. *You Can Negotiate Anything.* Mass Market Paperback, 1991.

Fisher, Roger and William Ury. *Getting to Yes.* Penguin Books, 1991.

Nierenberg, Gerard I. *The Complete Negotiator.* Barnes and Noble Books, 1996.

Princeton Review. *Negotiating Smart.* Crown Publishing Group, 1998.

Shell, G. Richard. *Bargaining for Advantage.* Penguin Books, 2000.

Ury, William. *Getting Past No.* Bantam Books, 1993.

PERSONAL INJURY CLAIM MANAGEMENT

Kaufman, William R. *How Insurance Companies Value Claims*. Costa Mesa, California: James Publishing, 1992.

Matthews, Joseph L. *How to Win Your Personal Injury Claim*. Berkeley, California: Nolo Press, 1996.

Miller, Clinton E. *How Insurance Companies Settle Cases*. Costa Mesa, California: James Publishing, 1994.

Rosen, Stephen J. *The Slip and Fall Handbook*. Columbia, Maryland: Hanrow Press, Inc., 1983.

Saperstein, Robert and Dana Saperstein. *Surviving an Auto Accident: A Guide to Your Physical, Economic and Emotional Recovery*. Ventura, California: Pathfinder Publishing of California, 1994.

Sarro, Joseph G. *There's No Mystery to Insurance Claims*. New York: Vantage Press, 1991.

SELF-AWARENESS AND SELF-MANAGEMENT

Fromm, Erich. *The Art of Being*. Continuum International, 1994.

Redfield, James. *The Celestine Vision: Living the New Spiritual Awareness*. Warner, 1997.

VanZant, Iyanlia. *Don't Give It Away: A Workbook of Self-Awareness and Self-Affirmation for Young Women*. Simon and Schuster, 1999.

Sanaya Roman, Orin. *Personal Power through Awareness*. Starseed Press, 1986.

Zukav, Gary. *The Heart of the Soul* (audio). Simon and Schuster, 2001.

APPENDIX B

Sample Engagement Agreements

TERMS AND CONDITIONS REGARDING
HOURLY ENGAGEMENT OF FIRM

1. **Matter**. Client retains Good, Better & Best, P.S. (Firm) and its attorneys to perform legal services for matter(s) identified herein:

The effective date for this agreement shall be _____.

2. **Relationship & Scope**.

2.1 **Prerequisites.** Upon execution of this engagement by Client and this firm, and payment of any required retainer, if any, this firm is thereafter retained to act as Client's attorney and agent within the scope of our engagement.

2.2 **Scope.** Client empowers the firm to take or cause to be taken all steps in connection with this matter deemed advisable by the firm, including but not limited to the investigation of the facts, the institution and pursuit of appropriate legal and/or administrative proceedings, lawsuits and negotiations in connection with the settlement or resolution of the matter.

3. **Compensation.**

3.1 **Hourly Rates**. This firm generates its fee by charging for the time expended by the professional. Professional services by attorneys are charged at hourly rates specified as follows:

Partner $ _____ per hour

Associate $ _____ per hour

Paralegal $ _____ per hour

The minimum time charge is two-tenths of an hour (.2) for phone calls and three-tenths of an hour (.3) for letters. Hourly rates are revised periodically and prospectively, but generally on an annual basis. Revised rates will apply to services rendered after the date of revision. As an alternative, in whole or in part, to hourly rate billing, the firm also reserves the right to charge fees on the basis of standardized fixed-fee billing charges or value billing for document production and delineated legal services. If the firm begins charging on such a basis, in whole or in part, the client shall be provided with documentation supporting such service charges.

3.2. **Reasonable Fee**. Lawyers use time and billing rates only as a guide in determining a reasonable fee for services rendered. Utilizing factors set forth in applicable professional rules, the standard we employ is whether a lawyer of ordinary prudence would be left with a definite and firm conviction that the fee being charged is above or below the range of fees which would be considered reasonable. In our sole judgment, if (1) our proposed fee exceeds the reasonable range of fees, we will reduce it, or (2) if our fee is unreasonably low, we reserve the option to raise the fee. If you disagree with our assessment of a reasonable fee, you are encouraged to discuss the matter with the responsible attorney, bring it to the attention of the Office Manager, or as a last resort, you are entitled to arbitrate any fee dispute through our bar association or through private arbitration services. You will be responsible for paying your share of any arbitration fees or costs.

4. **Entire Agreement.** This engagement letter comprises the entire agreement between the parties and the terms hereof shall not be modified except by written instrument executed by all parties hereto.

5. **Delegation.** The attorney signing this agreement will not necessarily be the sole or primary timekeeper/attorney assigned to the matter. This firm delegates certain types of matters to other attorneys or paralegals in the firm with experience in similar types of cases. On occasion, we may employ contract attorneys or associate with other attorneys in other firms to assist in the representation of the client. It is understood that you will extend your full cooperation to all members and staff of this firm, contract attorneys and associate counsel. If you object to this actual or potential delegation, you should immediately notify the undersigned attorney in writing. The firm reserves the right to withdraw if delegation, in whole or in part, is prohibited by the client.

6. **Absence of Warranties/Guarantees.** Client understands that Attorneys do not and cannot guarantee success or any particular result in matters assigned to the firm. While we shall use our best professional efforts to achieve a successful result, we can make no warranty as to the successful termination of this matter in your favor. An expression of the relative merits of your claims and chances of success are only expressions of legal opinion and educated estimates.

7. **Settlement or Compromise.** Attorneys shall not negotiate, settle, nor compromise Client's claim or position without Client's consent and approval. Any agreement negotiated on behalf of Client is subject to approval by Client. However, once you authorize us to settle or agree to a negotiated term or condition, you acknowledge that settlement is binding upon you.

8. **Retainer**. This firm generally requires an advance retainer to be deposited before we accept responsibility for this case. The initial retainer required is set forth on the last page of this letter. All monies received as retainer shall be deposited in firm's trust account to be disbursed for costs and disbursements as needed and for fees for attorneys' services as earned under any flat-fee or hourly rate agreements. Client and firm agree to review client's account as needed to determine whether the initial retainer remains sufficient to cover anticipated costs and fees. Client agrees, upon firm's request, to make additional deposits to the trust account as shall periodically appear necessary to cover anticipated costs and/or fees. The retainer deposit is not an estimate of the total projected cost of this engagement.

9. **Costs**. In addition to arrangements for legal service fees, you will be expected to reimburse the firm for all costs advanced and expenses incurred by the firm for your matter(s). Without limitation, these costs may include expenses for investigation, service of process, filing or recording fees, expert fees, depositions, messenger, postage, photocopies ($.20 per copy), fax charges ($.25 per page), long-distance telephone charges ($.25 per minute), travel and per diem expense, auto travel, and similar out-of-pocket expenses. Computerized legal research services, if used for Client, will be billed separately at the CALR vendor's charge without markup, in addition to the hourly charge for professional services. Clients are required to pay costs as incurred and billed.

10. **Monthly Billing**. We bill periodically with invoices and statements as part of our efforts to keep you informed about your case and its financial status. Our ability to provide legal services is dependent upon our clients' timely payment for such services. THE INVOICE OR STATEMENT BALANCE FOR COSTS AND FEES FOR LEGAL SERVICES, IF ANY, AND

OTHER CHARGEABLE EXPENSES ARE PAYABLE WITHIN 10 DAYS AFTER PRESENTATION OF STATEMENTS. If statements remain unpaid and/or a mutually acceptable agreement is not reached, we will be forced to withdraw as your attorneys. In all cases, a late charge of no more than one percent (1%) per month will be imposed on any balance not paid by the beginning of the next billing cycle. If funds belonging to you come into our possession, we are authorized to deduct our earned fees and costs from such funds prior to disbursement of the balance of the funds to you. Even if client seeks reimbursement of fees from third parties, client remains responsible for timely payment of statement balances.

11. **Enforcement/Venue**. In the event that either party is required to enforce the financial terms of this agreement, it is understood that the prevailing party with respect to financial performance hereunder shall be entitled to an award of reasonable attorneys' fees and costs. All disputes arising under this engagement letter, either professional or financial, shall be subject to binding arbitration in lieu of litigation. Absent contrary agreement by the parties, such arbitration shall be conducted in accordance with the Superior Court Rules and Rules of Evidence (ER) and arbitration statutes. The arbitrator shall be selected from the American Arbitration Association panel. The parties agree to limit the number of arbitrators to one person mutually agreed to by the parties, or if agreement is unreachable, by the Superior Court. This agreement shall be construed in accordance with the laws of the state of residence of the attorneys. Venue for any arbitration or suit shall be in the county in which Good, Better and Best maintain their main office.

12. **Attorneys' Right to Withdraw**. Attorneys may withdraw at any time if Client's financial obligations set out in this Agreement

are not met, if Client misrepresents or fails to disclose material facts, if Client fails to cooperate and/or assist in the handling of Client's matter, or for any other reasonable or compelling circumstance. Withdrawal does not waive the Client's obligation to pay fees and costs incurred to the effective date of withdrawal. The firm shall be entitled to photocopy the Client's file and retain such copied portions of the Client's file as the firm sees fit for its records. All balances shall be paid upon withdrawal.

13. **Client's Right to Discharge Attorneys**. Client may terminate Attorneys' services at any time, with or without cause, by notice in writing. Such termination does not discharge Client's obligation to pay all costs and fees charged or incurred up to and including the effective date of termination. The firm shall be entitled to photocopy the Client's file and retain such copied portions of the Client's file as the firm sees fit for its records. All fees and costs are due upon withdrawal or termination.

14. **Employment of Experts and Investigators.** Attorney, in its discretion or with client's approval, may employ professional, engineering, technical, or medical experts or investigators, as required, to examine, investigate, and report to attorney the facts regarding any element of the claim or case. All such experts or investigators shall report exclusively to Attorney for the purpose of preserving the "work-product" character of the information. Fees charged by such experts and investigators shall be charged to the client as costs under paragraph nine (9).

15. **Payment for Contract Attorneys and Associate Counsel.** Attorney may, in its discretion, utilize legal counsel outside of the firm to assist the Attorney either as co-counsel or as contract attorneys. The fees for such associate or contract counsel shall be a chargeable fee to the client under this agreement.

16. **Payment of Third-party Costs and Fees.** In the event of any financial recovery on behalf of the Client, and to the extent that funds are available from the Client's portion of recovery after deduction of this firm's earned fees and costs, the Client authorizes this firm to pay directly from such available funds all known outstanding balances owed to experts, investigators, providers, and/or any person who provided services or products relative to the case/matter. Such payments shall be made before disbursing any remaining balance to the Client. In the event of a billing or payment dispute, any sums in dispute shall be retained in the Attorney's trust account without accrual of interest until consistent instructions for disbursement are received from the Client and any third party; or at the request of the Client, deposited into the registry of the court having jurisdiction over the dispute by way of an interpleader action. Any filing fees or service fees arising by virtue of such an interpleader action shall be reimbursed to the firm by the Client.

REQUIRED RETAINER: $

APPROVED AND ACCEPTED:

CLIENT:

By: _____ Date:_____

Print Name:_____

By: _____ Date:_____

Print Name:_____

GOOD, BETTER & BEST, P.S.

_____ Date:_____

David Y. B. Good, President

CLIENT ENGAGEMENT AGREEMENT

(Contingent Fee)

This is an agreement that establishes a professional relationship between the firm of Good, Better & Best, P.S. (Firm) and the undersigned Client (and/or a minor in Client's household for whom Client is the parent or guardian) who has suffered a personal injury and seeks assistance from this firm as Client's representative in obtaining compensation for the injuries sustained. The scope of our engagement is to assist the Client in his or her financial recovery.

1. *Employment of Attorneys.*

1.1 Upon the signing of this agreement, you, as the Client or as the personal representative or guardian of the Client, employ this firm as your attorney to act on your behalf by investigating, negotiating, and if necessary, litigating your claim for damages as a result of a personal injury sustained by you or a minor or person for whom you are guardian or parent. You agree that in employing this firm, several of the firm's personnel will be involved in the tasks of this case, and, as a result, more than one attorney may be involved in representing you. The attorney executing this agreement will remain the attorney primarily responsible for your case. It is critical to the professional relationship fashioned by this agreement that you be candid and forthright in discussing the details of your case with the attorney representing you. All conversations between you and the professionals of this firm are strictly confidential and are privileged from compulsory disclosure.

1.2 Because facts are not necessarily available to the firm at the time of engagement by the Client, the firm reserves the right to investigate the Client's claim and make a decision regarding continued representation by the firm based upon the facts and circumstances revealed by our investigation. This determination will be made within a reasonable time after the completion of the investigation, and a written decision will be provided to the Client thereafter.

2. *Fee Structure.* The billing for this matter will involve two types of items—(1) "Fees," the amount due for the attorney's services and the services of other professionals within the firm, and (2) "Costs," the expenses for the services of outside consultants or vendors, and any out-of-pocket expenses of the firm, including such items as messenger or process-server fees, investigators, filing fees, recording fees, medical-record fees, postage, copying charges ($.20 per page), expert-witness fees, court-reporter fees for depositions, travel expense, parking and mileage fees, facsimile transmission charges ($2.00 first page, $.50 second and subsequent pages), and a file-opening fee of $25. Computer online research costs shall be assessed to the client by the firm without markup based upon the vendor's per-minute charge and any vendor surcharges. This list is not necessarily all of the types of items which might occur in your case as costs.

3. *Payment of Fees and Costs.*

3.1 *Costs.* You agree to reimburse the firm for all costs it incurs on your behalf as your agent in this matter. The firm will advance costs in its discretion and may require expenses and advances to be paid by the Client. At the option of the firm, arrangements for the payment of costs may be required prior to trial. Unless a decision is made to require pre-payment, you are encouraged, but not required, to pay all or part of these costs on a monthly basis as they are billed to you. Unpaid costs will incur a monthly late charge of one percent (1%). In all events, these costs will be paid from any proceeds arising from preliminary legal work or at the final resolution of the matter. Regardless of the outcome, however, you remain responsible to reimburse the firm for the costs incurred.

3.2 *Fees*. You also agree to pay this firm one-third (33.33%) of the amount recovered for you. Unless otherwise excluded herein, the "amount recovered" includes all sums paid to you as a result of this firm's representation of you and negotiation on your behalf including PIP, UIM/UM, property damage, or a third party's insurance coverage. "Amount recovered" also excludes any award of sanctions or attorneys' fees for services rendered by this firm. In the event that attorneys' fees are awarded to the Client or this firm, such an award shall be allocated solely to the law firm, except such an award shall be credited on a dollar-for-dollar basis against any fee recovery that would otherwise accrue by virtue of any Client recovery in the case. No separate attorney-fee recovery, independent of any contingent-fee recovery, shall be payable to the Client. Property damage or PIP recoveries are not included unless this firm is required to enter negotiations, arbitrate, or litigate to recover such sums. Should there be no financial recovery in this matter for you, there will be no additional fee to you for the professional services of the attorneys and other firm professionals.

3.3 *Structured Settlement*. If there is a settlement of Client's case, the settlement may be partially in immediate cash and partially in future periodic payments to the Client. Client hereby authorizes attorney to satisfy the fees and costs owed attorney under this agreement from the immediate cash portion of such settlement and not from the periodic payment's portion. Client further agrees that attorney may receive the fees owed attorney under this agreement in future periodic payments in amounts and at time to be negotiated immediately prior to settlement when the fee shall be earned. Those future periodic payments may not be pro rata with future periodic payments of the Client. Nevertheless, the present value of any such deferred fees on the date of settlement shall not exceed the percentage set forth in this paragraph of the present value of all amounts to be paid in the settlement.

4. *Employment of Experts, Investigators or Other Counsel.* You authorize this firm to hire and retain such experts or investigators as shall be required in the discretion of the responsible attorney to examine, investigate, and report to the attorney certain facts regarding an element of this case. The firm will seek your approval before retaining any expert witness. Fees for such experts or investigators shall be charged to you as costs, and billed periodically.

In the discretion of the responsible attorney, you authorize this firm to retain and utilize legal counsel outside the firm to assist the responsible attorney. Such legal counsel may be independent lawyers working under contract to the firm, or be associated as co-counsel and work at other firms. Unless otherwise agreed, the fee of such outside counsel shall be included within the contingent fee due this firm and shall not be an added expense for you.

In addition, in some cases, when a client comes to the firm through the recommendation of another attorney, a fee is paid to that attorney proportionally to the work performed for doing the initial work-up for a case, or for remaining jointly responsible for the case outcome in accordance with the applicable rules of professional conduct. In the event any such arrangement occurs in this case, the identity of such recommending attorney shall be set forth at the bottom of this letter. The Client should advise the firm of any objection or concern over this fee. Such fees are included within the existing contingent fee structure and do not represent an additional cost to the Client.

5. *Settlement or Compromise.*

5.1 *Authority to Settle.* This is your case. Prior to any settlement, your approval for any settlement will first be obtained. Once resolved on your behalf, the settlement will be binding upon you. Monies recovered and paid to you are subject to later audit for mathematical errors or omitted costs, subrogation interests, or other liabilities properly payable by you. In the event of an omitted item, you will be responsible for payment from your disbursement. In the event that funds are disbursed to you subject to an outstanding subrogation claim left unresolved at the time of settlement, you understand that payment of that subrogation claim or other lien will be made out of your portion of the settlement funds, and this firm will be held harmless by you from payment or claim of such subrogation or lien.

5.2 *Disbursement.* Prior to distribution of any recovery to you, there will be deducted monies owed to subrogated interests and providers. Subrogation interests are any monies owed to insurance companies or others who have paid funds to you and have a claim against any funds ultimately recovered from a third party. We will also deduct from your share of the recovery the bills of your healthcare providers who have agreed to await the outcome of your case before seeking payment. In the event that a dispute arises with respect to any subrogation claim or provider claim, you authorize to either (1) retain the disputed amount in our trust account pending resolution of the dispute between you or the subrogated party or provider or (2) at our discretion, deposit the disputed amounts into the registry of the court by the way of an interpleader action and (3) in either event, to direct the contestants to resolve their dispute informally or formally in the court without further participation by this firm. You further consent to the deposit of funds received from settlement, award, or satisfaction of judgment into the firm's trust account and waive any interest that may otherwise accrue pending clearance of such funds and their distribution to you.

At the time of settlement disbursement, a security deposit of not less than $250.00 will also be withheld from the payment to you for a period of approximately 60 days to pay for any costs that were unbilled at the time of the final payment to you of the amount recovered.

You authorize us to make a series of payments from the gross amount recovered in any settlement, including (1) payment of our contingent fee, (2) reimbursement to this firm of any costs advanced by the firm, (3) payment to any undisputed subrogated interests of amounts due them for funds previously advanced to you or on your behalf, (4) payment of the undisputed liens or billings of any health care providers who provided you health-care or other services in this matter, and (5) the unbilled cost deposit discussed above.

To assist you in computing this recovery, the following worksheet is supplied as an example:

Gross amount recovered	$_____
Less Firm's Fee (33.33%)	($_____)
Subtotal	$_____
Less Unpaid Firm Costs	($_____)
Less Subrogated Interests or Liens	($_____)
Less Unpaid Healthcare Provider Bills	($_____)
Less Temporary Cost Deposit	($___500.00)*
Net Recovery to You	$_____

(*) The cost deposit covers any outstanding obligations that have not been billed or known at the time of settlement and disbursement.

6. *Absence of Guarantee of Recovery*. This firm cannot and does not guarantee any amount of recovery for you in your case.

7. *Termination of Professional Relationship*. You have the right to change attorneys to another attorney or firm at any time by sending us a letter to that effect. This right to discharge this firm as your representative requires that you remain responsible for all costs incurred prior to receipt of your letter and for payment at the time of settlement or collection of a judgment or verdict to this firm of a fee for professional services in an amount equivalent to the time expended on your case at the usual hourly rate for the attorney or other professionals involved. Our usual hourly rate for attorneys varies from $165 to $400, depending upon experience, and from $65 to $115 for paralegals, depending upon experience.

Likewise, this firm may choose to withdraw from representing you and request, in writing, that you obtain another attorney or firm to represent you. As with a discharge, a withdrawal by this firm does not relieve you of the responsibility to pay costs and the fees for professional services to this firm at the time of settlement or collection of a judgment or verdict in an amount equivalent to the time expended on your case at the usual hourly rate for the attorney or other professionals involved.

In the event that a discharge or withdrawal occurs after the firm substantially completes its representation of your matter and settlement occurs within a reasonable period thereafter, the firm retains its right to seek payment of its contingent fee.

8. *Physician/Patient Privileged Information*. While normally anything you tell your physician is privileged and confidential,

state law may require that you waive this privilege of confidentiality, allowing the defendant's counsel to examine your medical records and question your physician as to this matter without further consent by you. By authorizing us to file litigation in this matter, you are acknowledging that you understand that one consequence of filing the litigation will be examination by opposing counsel and their experts of your medical records.

9. *Entire Agreement and Dispute Resolution.* This agreement is the complete agreement between the firm and you with respect to establishing and maintaining the professional relationship and fee distribution structure. Any changes to this agreement must be in writing signed by both parties. In the event of a dispute as to the agreements and promises contained in this agreement, you have the option to petition the court in which your personal injury claim was litigated within 45 days of the receipt of the final billing or accounting to have the court determine the reasonableness of the contingent fee charged in your case. Any other dispute shall be resolved by arbitration in accordance with the American Arbitration Association. In the event that any dispute leads to arbitration or litigation between the parties regarding financial aspects of this relationship, the prevailing party shall be entitled to attorneys' fees and costs. The provision of attorneys' fees does not pertain to claims of professional misconduct or malpractice.

Executed by the parties on this _____day of _____, 20____

CLIENT

By: _____

Print Name: _____

Good, Better & Best, P.S.

By: _____

David Y. B. Good, President

APPENDIX C

INTERNET LEGAL RESOURCES

(See www.peick-usa.com for a variety of legal, healthcare, and business Web links)

ATTORNEYS

Martindale-Hubbell
Attorneys purchase ad space in this publication. Searchable by attorney, firm, location, type of practice, etc.
http://lawyers.martindale.com/marhub/form?_form=attorney.html

West's Legal Directory
Attorneys purchase ad space in this publication. Searchable by attorney, firm, location, type of practice, etc.
http://www.wld.com/ldsearch.htm

ATTORNEY BAR ASSOCIATIONS

American Bar Association (ABA) Bar Links
Links to international, national, state, and local bar associations
http://www.abanet.org/lawlink/associations.html

LEGAL—FEDERAL

United States Constitution
Searchable, annotated
http://www.findlaw.com/casecode/constitution

United States Code
Searchable and maintained by Cornell Law School
http://www.law.cornell.edu/uscode/

Code of Federal Regulations

Searchable, maintained by National Archives
Administration
http://www.law.cornell.edu/uscode/

THOMAS

Bills pending in Congress, committee reports, and
Congressional Record
http:/thomas.loc.gov/

U.S. Supreme Court Opinions

Opinions since 1893, searchable by party or opinion text
http://www.findlaw.com/casecode/supreme.html

Federal Rules of Civil Procedure

Rules in hypertext format from Cornell Law School
http://www.law.cornell.edu/rules/frcp/overview.html

Federal Rules of Evidence

Rules in hypertext format from Cornell Law School
http://www.law.cornell.edu/rules/fre/overview.html

GPO Search Pages

Search Federal Register, CFR, Congressional Record, etc.
http://www.access.gpo.gov/su_docs/aces/special.html

Federal Web Locator

Links and searches for federal Web resources
http:/www.law.vill.edu/Fed-Agency/fedwebloc.html

U.S House Law Library

Links to federal Web resources
http://law.house.gov

FedWorld

Searchable governmental directory to federal Web sites
http://www.fedworld.gov/

LEGAL—GENERAL MATERIALS

CataLaw Metaindex
Searchable legal resources by topic or region
http://www.catalaw.com/

Cornell Legal Information Institute
Links to Web legal resources by topic; considerable
online content http://www.law.cornell.edu

FindLaw
Excellent starting point for locating materials on many
legal issues http://www.findlaw.com

Findlaw Legal Minds
View postings to many listserv discussion groups
http://www.legalminds.org

Law-related Listservs
A guide to choosing and using law-related listservs
http://www.regent.edu/lawlib/lists/list-law.html

List Tool Subscription Manager
Subscribe to many law-related listservs from a single
location
http:// www.lawguru.com/subscribe/listtool.html

Findlaw Legal Forms
Links to legal forms on a variety of subjects
http://www.findlaw.com/16forms/index.html

W3 Lawyer
Searchable Web resources organized by legal subject area
http://www.njlawnet.com/w3lawyer

APPENDIX D

Internet Non-Legal Resources for Consumers

AUTOMOTIVE INFORMATION AND VALUATIONS

Edmunds.com

Edmunds has transferred its many written guidebooks onto the Internet and operates a website with an incredibly vast amount of information on new and used vehicles and their values. See http://www.edmunds.com

INSURANCE

National Consumers League
815 15th Avenue NW
Washington, DC 20005
202-639-8140

Insurance Information Institute
110 William Street
New York, NY 10038
800-221-4954

National Insurance Helpline
800-942-4242

Insurance Crime Prevention Institute
15 Franklin Street
Westport, CT 06880
800-221-5715

DRINKING AND DRIVING

Citizens for Safe Drivers
P.O. Box 42018
Washington, DC 20015
301-469-6282

Mothers Against Drunk Driving
511 East John Carpenter Frwy, Suite 700
Irving, TX 75062
800-GET-MADD

National Clearinghouse for Alcohol and Drug Information
P.O. Box 2345
Rockville, MD 20852

HIGHWAY SAFETY

Insurance Institute for Highway Safety
10005 N Glebe Road
Arlington, VA 22201
703-247-1500

National Highway Traffic Safety Administration
400 Seventh Street SW
Washington, DC 20590
202-366-9588

National Safety Council
444 North Michigan Avenue
Chicago, IL 60611
312-527-4800

VICTIM ORGANIZATIONS

National Organization for Victim Assistance (NOVA)
1757 Park Road NW
Washington, DC 20010
202-232-6682

APPENDIX E

STATE BAR ASSOCIATIONS

Alphabetical by state

Alabama State Bar
415 Dexter Avenue
Montgomery, AL 36104
334-269-1515
334-261-6310 (fax)
www.alabar.org

Alaska Bar Association
P.O. Box 100279
510 L Street Suite 602
Anchorage, AK 99501
907-272-2932(fax)
www.alaskabar.org
info@alaskabar.org

Arizona State Bar Association
111 West Monroe Suite 1800
Phoenix, AZ 85003-1742
602-271-4930 (fax)
www.azbar.org
azbar@azbar.org

Arkansas Bar Association
400 West Markham
Little Rock, AR 72201
800-609-5668
www.arkbar.org
arkbar1@swbell.net

State Bar of California
180 Howard Street
San Francisco, CA 94105-1639
415-538-2000
www.calbar.org

Colorado Bar Association
1900 Grant Street, Ninth Floor
Denver, CO 80203
303-860-1115
303-894-0821 (fax)
www.cobar.org

Delaware State Bar Association
301 North Market Street
Wilmington, DE 19801
302-658-5279
302-658-5212 (fax)
www.dsba.org

Bar Association of the District
of Columbia
1819 H Street NW 12th Floor
Washington, DC 20006
202-223-6600
202-293-3388 (fax)
www.badc.org

The Florida Bar
650 Apallachee Parkway
Tallahassee, FL 32399-2300
850-561-5600
www.flabar.org

State Bar of Georgia
800 The Hurt Building
50 Hurt Plaza
Atlanta, GA 30303
404-527-8700
www.gabar.org

Hawaii State Bar Association
1132 Bishop Street #906

Honolulu, HI 96813
808-537-1868
808-521-7936 (fax)
www.hsba.org

Idaho State Bar
P.O. Box 895
Boise, ID 83701
208-334-4500
208-334-4515
www.www2.state.id.us/isb/

Illinois State Bar
Illinois Bar Center
Springfield, IL 62701-1779
217-525-1760
www.illinoisbar.org

Indiana State Bar Association
230 East Ohio Street 4th Floor
Indianapolis, IN 46204
317-639-5465 or 317-268-2588
isbaadmin@inbar.org
www.inbar.org

Iowa State Bar
521 East Locust 3rd Floor
Des Moines, IA 50309
515-243-3179
www.iowabar.org

Kansas Bar Association
1200 SW Harrison Street
Topeka, KS 66612-1806
785-234-5696
www.ksbar.org

Louisiana State Bar Association
601 St. Charles Avenue
New Orleans, LA 70130-3404
504-566-1600
www.lsba.org

Maine State Bar Association
124 State Street
P.O. Box 788
Augusta, ME 04332-0788
207-622-7523
info@mainebar.org
www.mainebar.org

Maryland State Bar Association
520 West Fayette Street
Baltimore, MD 21201
410-685-7878
msba@msba.org
www.msba.org

Massachusetts Bar Association
20 West Street
Boston, MA 02111
617-338-0641

State Bar of Michigan
306 Townsend Street
Lansing, MI 48933-2083
517-346-6300
www.michbar.org

Minnesota State Bar Association
600 Nicollet Mall #380
Minneapolis, MN 55402
612-333-1183
www2.mnbar.org

The Mississippi Bar
P.O. Box 2168
643 North State Street
Jackson, MS 39225-2168
601-948-4471
601-355-8635 (fax)
http://msbar.org

The Missouri Bar
P.O. Box 119
Jefferson City, MO 65102
573-635-4128

Montana State Bar Association
46 North Last Chance Gulch #2A
Helena, MT 59624
406-442-7660 (fax
mailbox@montanabar.org
www.montanabar.org

Nebraska State Bar Association
635 South 14th Street
Lincoln, NE 68501
402-475-7091
www.nebar.com

Nevada: No organizations found

New Hampshire Bar Association
112 Pleasant Street
Concord, NH 03301
603-224-6942 (fax)
www.nhbar.org

New Jersey State Bar
New Jersey Law Center
One Constitution Square
New Brunswick, NJ 08901

State Bar of New Mexico
P.O. Box 25883
Albuquerque, NM 87125
505-797-6000, 505-828-3765
sbnm@nmbar.org
www.nmbar.org

New York State Bar Association
1 Elk Street
Albany, NY 12207
518-463-3200
www.nysba.org

North Carolina Bar Association
P.O. Box 3688
Cary, NCa 27519
919-677-0561(fax)
www.ncbar.org

North Dakota: Contact North Dakota Supreme Court

Ohio State Bar Association
1700 Lake Shore Drive
Columbus, OH 43204
800-282-6556
www.ohiobar.org

Oklahoma Bar Association
P.O. Box 53036
1901 N. Lincoln Boulevard
Oklahoma City, OK 73152-3036
www.okbar.org

Oregon State Bar
5200 SW Meadows Road
Lake Oswego, OR 97035
503-620-0222
www.osbar.org

Pennsylvania Bar Association
100 South Street
P.O. Box 186
Harrisburg, PA 17108-0186
717-238-6715 (fax)
www.pabar.org

Rhode Island Bar Association
115 Cedar Street
Providence, RI 02903
401-421-5740 (fax)
ribar@ids.net
www.ribar.org

South Carolina Bar Association
950 Taylor Street
Columbia, SC 29202
803-799-6653 (fax)
scbar-info@scbar.org
www.scbar.org

State Bar of South Dakota
222 East Capitol Avenue
Pierre, SD 57501-2596
605-224-7554
www.sdbar.org

Tennessee Bar Association
221 Fourth Avenue North Suite
400
Nashville, TN 37219
615-383-7421 (fax)
www.tba.org

State Bar of Texas
1414 Colorado
Austin, TX 78701
512-463-1463 (fax)
www.texasbar.com

Utah State Bar
645 South 200 East
Salt Lake City, Utah 84111
801-531-9077 (fax)
www.utahbar.org

Vermont Bar Association
P.O. Box 100
Montpelier, VT 05601-0100
802-223-2020 (fax)
www.vtbar.org

Virginia State Bar
707 East Main Street, Suite 1500
Richmond, VA 23219-2800
804-775-0500
www.vsb.org

Washington State Bar
Association
2101 Fourth Avenue, Fourth
Floor
Seattle, WA 98121-2330
206-443-WSBA (fax)
questions@wsba.org
www.wsba.org

West Virginia State Bar
2006 Kanawha Boulevard East
Charleston, WV 25311-2204
304-558-2456 (fax)
www.wvbar.org

State Bar of Wisconsin
P.O. Box 7158
Madison, Wisconsin 53707-7158
608-257-3838 (fax)
www.wisbar.org

Wyoming State Bar
500 Randall Avenue
Cheyenne, WY 82001
307-632-9061 (fax)
info@wyomingbar.org
www.wyomingbar.org

APPENDIX F

SAMPLE LITIGATION PLAN

Date _____

Proposed By: _____

Law Firm: _____

Claim #: _____

Caption: _____

Claim Associate: _____

Attorneys Assigned to Case: _____

_____

_____

Hourly Fee Rates:

Partner $_____

Associate $_____

Paralegal $_____

Contingent Fee (if applicable): $_____

Key Issues:

1. _____

2. _____

3. _____

4. _____

Specific Objective(s)

1. _____

2. _____

3. _____

Strategy: _____

_____

_____

PRE-LITIGATION OBJECTIVES:

Preliminary Activity	Projected Completion Date	Estimated Hours and Cost
Investigation of Facts		
Research Applicable Law		
Client Interviews		
Draft Demand Letter		
Negotiating Claims		

Subtotal—Preliminary Activity $_____

LITIGATION ACTIVITY required to achieve each specific objective. (Be specific: e.g., identify each deponent or recipient of discovery, type of motion, issue to be researched, etc. Use additional sheets as needed.)

Initial Pleading/ Preliminary Activity	Projected Completion Date	Estimated Hours and Cost
Summons and Complaint, if applicable		
Answer, if applicable		
Cross/Third-party Complaint		
Litigation Planning/ Budgeting		

Subtotal—Initial Pleading/Preliminary Activity $_____

Fact-finding/ Information Management	Project Completion Date	Estimated Hours and Cost
Written Discovery		
Depositions		
Interviews		
Document Management		
Expert Witness Interaction		
Review and Analysis		

Subtotal—Fact-finding/Information Management: $_____

Motion Practice	Projected Completion Date	Estimated Hours and Cost
Motion Research		
Draft Memoranda		
Court Conferences		
Review and Analysis		

Subtotal—Motion Practice and Pretrial Activity $_____

Communication	Projected Completion Date	Estimated Hours and Cost
Reporting		
Telephone		
Letters		
Conferences and Interoffice Communication		

Subtotal—Communication $ _____

Trial Activity	Projected Completion Date	Estimated Hours and Costs
Trial Preparation		
Trial Attendance		
Review and Analysis		
Court Conferences		

Subtotal—Trial Activity $_____

Expenses	Estimated Cost
Filing Fees	
External Copy Charges	
Internal Copy Charges	
Investigator Fees	
Lay Witness Expenses	
Expert Witness Fees	
Depositions	
Trial	
Travel and Lodging—Firm	
Travel and Lodging—Witnesses	
Deposition Transcription Charges	
Trial Exhibits	
Miscellaneous Expenses	

Subtotal—Expenses $ _____
Total Budget for Planned Activities $ _____

APPENDIX G

Deposition Guidelines

A discovery deposition in its simplest form is an opportunity for opposing counsel to explore all information held by a witness or party. A deposition is sworn testimony taken of a party or witness by a court reporter before trial. The purpose is to discover facts, obtain leads to other evidence, preserve testimony of a witness who may not be available at the time of trial, and establish a record of a witness's version of events, which may later be used to contradict the witness at trial if the witness changes that version of events. Your contribution to the deposition will be determined by your preparation, attitude, truthfulness, and appearance.

PREPARATION

Prior to the deposition, review all documents, reports, letters from your attorney, medical reports, the pleadings filed by your attorney, and any prior interrogatory answers you have provided your lawyer and, hence, opposing counsel. If you are missing any of these documents, contact your lawyer and get copies. Opposing counsel may ask you about these documents, and you must be familiar with them.

After this review, make an appointment with your lawyer to discuss the deposition. The timing and time allowed for this pre-deposition interview will vary with the case.

GUIDELINES

Tell the Truth. Tell the truth. You are under oath, and an intentionally false answer may constitute a crime. Falsehoods on the most minor or irrelevant points may be used to attack your credibility on more important issues. Be honest and as accurate as you are capable of being.

Dress Appropriately. Usually the first opportunity opposing counsel has to see you comes at the time of your deposition. It is important that you make a good impression. Appear at the deposition dressed as you would expect to dress if you were actually going to court.

Discuss Matters in Advance with Counsel. If you are concerned about something that might prove embarrassing or about something you have done relative to the issues in the case, discuss it candidly with your counsel before the deposition.

Do Not Bring Any Materials to the Deposition. Any materials you may wish to bring to the deposition should be specifically reviewed in advance by your counsel. Anything you review at the deposition, including personal notes, may be requested for examination by opposing counsel.

Do Not Be Influenced by the Examiner's Friendliness. Do not be concerned about rewarding the other lawyer for the kindness or concern shown to you; he's not doing it to help you.

Do Not Expand on the Story Unless Asked. Do not be concerned that all relevant facts have not been elicited by the examiner, or that the questions and answers create only a partial picture, unless such a picture is misleading or false. This is a discovery deposition, and your attorney may want to hold back some information for trial or later negotiations.

If you are not directly asked, do not volunteer. If your attorney believes the facts need expansion, he will ask you when it is his turn to speak. You will have an opportunity at trial to present additional testimony on matters not inquired about on the deposition.

Conference with Your Attorney and Breaks. If you wish to confer with your attorney, indicate that you wish to do so before being asked the next question. Most jurisdictions do not allow consultations while the question remains unanswered.

You may also confer during a break. Feel free to request a break if you feel tired or uncomfortable at any point. If your counsel suggests you need a break or indicates a desire to confer with you, always agree before proceeding with your testimony.

Off-the-record Discussions in the Deposition Room. If you have conversation with someone in the deposition room when the examiner is present, be prepared for questions on that conversation when you are "on the records." Be wary of any off-the-record discussion. Socializing is not required, only civility.

Be Courteous and Civil. Do not argue. Avoid any display of hostility. An effort may be made to provoke you in the hope that anger will cloud your judgment. Don't let this tactic succeed. Keep your temper.

Avoid Any Attempt at Levity or Sarcasm. It will appear you are not taking your oath seriously if you make jokes or wise cracks. Monitor your tone of voice because irony, sarcasm, and sadness are poorly reflected in the transcript and may convey the exact opposite impression from what was intended.

Avoid Derogatory Language. Avoid even the mildest obscenity and avoid absolutely any ethnic slurs or references, which could be considered derogatory. The transcript may be read back to a judge or jury who may take offense.

Do Not Make Promises. Don't agree to look up information, to obtain materials, to make calculations, etc., unless cleared first with your counsel.

Do Not Become Involved in Arguments of Counsel. Let your attorney handle the conversation. Trust his or her judgment about what needs to be discussed, and the ramifications of the disagreement.

Answer Only the Question That Is Asked. Do not anticipate questions. Do not volunteer information. Keep your answers short. Yes and no are satisfactory answers. When a short answer would be misleading, however, you have a right to explain your answer. If you don't know the answer, say only, "I don't know." If you cannot recall, say only, "I cannot recall at this time."

Speak Slowly, Clearly, and Audibly. This is important so that the court reporter will be able to take down every word. Let the examiner complete the questions before you begin to answer. Say "yes" rather than "uh-huh" and "no" rather than "uh-uh." Avoid nodding your head instead of audibly answering the question.

Listen Carefully to Each Question. Be sure you understand it entirely. Do not answer a question you do not understand. If you do not understand the question, say so. Do not hesitate to ask for clarification or for a rereading of the question.

Pause before Beginning Each Answer. Answer Slowly. This gives you time to reflect on the question, and it gives time to your counsel to formulate and interpose objections. The written transcript does not reflect how long you take to answer a question or how long you pause.

A deposition is not conversation, but rather a series of questions and answers. Give careful consideration to each question.

Stop answering immediately if your counsel starts talking. On complicated or difficult questions, you may state that you need time to consider before answering.

Listen Carefully to Objections. If an objection is raised to the question, listen to the objection very carefully. You may learn something about the dangers of the question from the objection. Give the lawyer the chance to complete the objection before you answer.

Where Appropriate, Qualify Your Answers. Use words such as, "To the best of my recollection," "As best I can recall," "My best recollection is," "I believe ..." Be as specific or vague as your memory allows. Where you are sure, do not hedge or unnecessarily weaken the force of a strong answer. If you are not sure, then you should indicate that you are not sure.

Pay Close Attention to the Question. Questions may contain facts, which you do not know to be true. Do not have the examiner put you in the position of adopting half-truths or unknown facts on which further questions may be based. Listen to the whole question; the examiner may tag something objectionable on the end.

Try Not to Answer Two Questions at Once. If the examiner asks you two questions, find out which one you should answer.

Indicate Whether You Are Paraphrasing or Quoting. In testifying regarding conversations, make it clear whether you are paraphrasing or quoting directly.

Avoid Absolutes Unless You Are Positive They Are Accurate. "Never" and "always" have a way of coming back to haunt you.

Do Not Guess or Offer an Opinion Unless Specifically Requested to Do So. If you do not know the answer, say so. If you have no personal knowledge, indicate that in your answer. Do not venture or guess or offer an opinion unless it is specifically called for and then only after giving your counsel an opportunity to object.

Stay with What You Know. Do not hesitate to say that you do not know. Do not volunteer who might know.

As Long As You Are Satisfied with Your Answer, Do Not Be Concerned Whether the Examiner Understands or Seems to Understand What You Are Saying. There is a transcript of the deposition, and your answer may be reviewed in writing at any time. Less is often better.

If You Are Interrupted, Say So. Let the lawyer finish the interruption and then firmly but courteously state that you were interrupted, that you had not finished your answer to the previous question, and then complete your answer. You may ask to have the question and answer read back if that would be helpful to allow you to collect your thoughts.

Do Not Feel Compelled to Speak Simply Because There Is a Moment of Silence. Sometimes, after you give an answer, there will be silence. The other lawyer may be thinking how to word the next question. Silence sometimes makes a witness uncomfortable. You may be tempted to fill the silence with words. Don't. Keep quiet and wait.

If Advised Not to Answer by Your Counsel, Do Not Answer Even if You Believe the Answer Would Be Helpful. If you feel the advice was erroneous, request a break to confer with counsel.

If You Realize That Your Earlier Answer Was in Error or Incomplete, You May Correct or Supplement It. You should not say that an earlier answer is true if you become aware that it is not.

If Asked about a Document, Read It Carefully before You Begin to Answer. If you do not recall the document or do not know to an absolute certainty exactly what the document says or what its author meant, say so. Don't guess at what may have been meant.

Expect to Be Asked What You Have Done and What Files You Have Examined in Preparation for Your Deposition. This includes any financial arrangements concerning your appearance. Discuss this subject with counsel before the deposition.

Do Not Worry about Whether Your Answer Helps or Hurts Your Case. You have enough to do in concentrating on the accuracy of your testimony in order to preserve your credibility at trial. There is usually some good and some bad in every case.

PHYSICAL APPEARANCE

- Be clean and well groomed.
- Avoid jewelry or expensive ornamentation.
- Dress conservatively.
- Males should wear white or light blue shirts, conservative ties, and suits or sport-coat combinations of blue or gray. Avoid wide pin stripes and loud colors and patterns.
- Males should get a haircut and trim any mustaches and beards.
- Females should dress in either conservative business fashions or subdued dress. Avoid casual or party attire.

Keeping the above in mind, avoid creating too severe an image.

- Sit upright and avoid slouching. Do not fidget. Pay attention to your body language and hand movements to avoid inadvertent cues that you are nervous or uncertain about your case.

APPENDIX H

GLOSSARY OF LEGAL TERMS

Understanding the language of the law is equally important to understanding your attorney. This glossary provides general definitions for legal terms. These definitions are intended primarily to help you to understand what you read in this field guide. These definitions are not intended to be comprehensive and do not replace definitions found in statutes, regulations, cases, and similar resources.

A

abrogate: To abolish or annul a former law by legislative act or constitutional authority.

abstract: A summarized record of the actions taken by a court or other governmental agency.

abstract of judgment: Summary of the final decision of a court. May be filed with the county recorder to serve as a lien.

accomplice: A person who knowingly and willingly assists the principal offender in the commission of a crime.

accused: A person or persons against whom a criminal proceeding is initiated. (See also **defendant**.)

acknowledgment: The act of declaring, testifying, or certifying that something is genuine. This can be done orally or in writing.

acquittal: The legal finding by a judge or jury that the accused is not guilty.

action: A court proceeding when one party prosecutes another for the protection or enforcement of a right, the prevention or correction of a wrong, or the punishment of an offense.

ad hoc vice: The status of an attorney not licensed in a particular state who is allowed to practice in the state for only a single case.

adjournment: The act of postponing a court session to another time or place. (See also **continuance** and **recess**.)

adjudication: The judgment or decision of the court or jury regarding a case or cause of action.

ad litem: For the purpose of the suit; from the Latin for "for the suit."

admonition to jury: A statement given by a judge to a panel of jurors advising them of (1) their duty and expected conduct as jurors, (2) the admissibility or non-admissibility of evidence, and (3) the purpose for which admitted evidence may be considered.

adverse witness: A person called to testify by the other side of the litigation.

affidavit: A written statement of facts sworn to under oath in the presence of someone legally authorized to administer it, e.g., judge, notary public.

affirm: To make a solemn declaration or oath (used when a person does not want to swear to the truth of something).

affirmation: A finding by an appellate court that the judgment of a lower court is correct and should stand. (See also **uphold**.)

affirmative defense: A defense that serves as a basis for providing some new fact; in such a defense, defendant does not simply deny a charge but offers new evidence to avoid judgment against him or her; defendant must raise the defense in the answer and has the burden of proof on defense.

amicus curiae: A person invited to advise a court on a matter of law in a case to which he or she is not a party; from the Latin for "friend of the court."

annulment (nullity of marriage): A legal action that says a marriage was never legally valid because of unsound mind, incest, bigamy, being under the age of consent, fraud, force, or physical incapacity.

answer: The formal written statement by a defendant responding to a civil complaint and setting forth the grounds for his or her defense.

appeal: A request made after a trial by a party who has lost on one or more issues that a higher (appellate) court review the trial court's decision to determine if it was correct. To make such a request is "to appeal" or "to take an appeal." One who appeals is called the "appellant," the other party is the "appellee."

appearance: The formal act of presenting oneself physically to the jurisdiction of a court; a document identifying representing counsel.

appellate court: A court having jurisdiction to review the law as applied in a prior determination of the same case. (See also **trial court**.)

arbitration: A process in which a neutral person or persons review evidence, hear arguments, and render a decision regarding a dispute.

arraignment: A proceeding in which an individual who is accused of committing a crime is brought into court, told of the charges, and asked to plead guilty or not guilty.

arrest: The legal apprehension of a person charged with a crime.

assault: A threat or attempt to do bodily harm that falls short of actual battery; may or may not include physical violence.

attachment: (1) Document attached to court papers to provide additional information; (2) mode of collecting judgment by taking property by court order.

attorney: A person qualified to represent clients in a court of law and to advise them on legal matters.

attorney of record: An attorney whose name is in the permanent case record as representing a party in an action.

B

backlog: A total inventory of cases that have not reached disposition within mandated timeframes.

bail bond: A document purchased from a bondsman that is given to the court instead of money for bail. Once signed by the defendant, he or she is released from custody on the condition that the amount stated on the bail bond will be forfeited should the defendant not appear in court at the required time.

bail exoneration: The refund of a bail deposit to the depositor or the release of his or her liability to a surety company.

bail forfeiture: The retention by court order of a bail deposit for failure to appear in court at an appointed time.

bailiff: A court attendant assigned by a sheriff, marshal, or constable to provide security to the court.

bankruptcy: A legal process by which persons or businesses that cannot pay their debts can seek the assistance of the court in getting a fresh start. Under the protection of the bankruptcy court, debtors may discharge their debts, usually by paying a portion of each debt. Bankruptcy judges preside over these proceedings.

battery: Any unlawful beating or other wrongful physical violence or constraint inflicted on a person without his or her consent.

bench trial: Trial without a jury in which a judge decides which party prevails; also called a court trial.

bench warrant: A written order issued by the court from the judge (or "bench") commanding a person's arrest.

bind over: A finding at a preliminary examination in a trial court that sufficient evidence exists against the defendant to require a trial.

bona fide: Made without fraud or deceit; sincere, genuine; from the Latin for "in or with good faith."

bond: A deed or instrument that binds, restrains, or obligates a person. In the courts, a bond is a written statement that obligates one person to pay a specified amount of money to another person.

book (booking): A process performed by police at the time of arrest that involves fingerprinting, photographing, and writing down personal data about a suspect.

breath test: A chemical analysis of someone's breath to determine the percentage of alcohol fumes present.

brief: A written statement submitted by each party in a case that explains why the court should decide the case, or particular issues in a case, in that party's favor.

burden of proof: The duty of a party to produce the greater amount of evidence on a point at issue in a case.

C

calendar: An alphabetical, categorized list of each case to be heard in each courtroom every day. "To calendar a case" means to assign a day, time, and courtroom to it.

capital case: A criminal case in which death may be the punishment.

capital offense: A crime punishable by death.

caption: A heading on all pleadings submitted to the court. It states information such as the case name, court, and case number.

case: A lawsuit; also used to describe any complaint filed in the criminal, traffic, or civil division of a court.

case law: Law established by the history of judicial decisions in cases.

case number: Number assigned by the court clerk's office to identify a particular case. This number appears on all other documents filed in the case.

cause of action: The charges (or "counts") that make the basis for a case or lawsuit.

challenge for cause: Reasons given by an attorney to support a request that a potential juror or judge be removed from service on a particular case. (Compare **peremptory challenge**.)

chambers: A judge's office, typically including work space for the judge's clerks.

change of venue: The transfer of a civil or criminal case from one judicial district to another.

chattel: An article of personal property.

citation: An order or summons notifying a defendant/respondent of the charges being made and commanding the defendant to appear in court and/or post bail.

civil case: An action brought by a person or party to recover property, to force someone to honor a contract, or to protect one's civil rights.

civil jurisdiction: The authority, capacity, power, or right of a court to hear non-criminal matters.

claim splitting: Dividing a civil claim and filing two lawsuits to stay below the limits on amounts of claims. Claim splitting is prohibited in most cases.

codicil: A supplement or amendment to a will.

commissioner: A person appointed by the court who is given the power to hear and make decisions concerning certain limited legal matters.

common law: The body of law derived from judicial decisions, rather than from statutes or constitutions.

compensatory damages: The amount of money to be paid by one person to another that covers only the actual cost or equivalent cost of the wrong or injury caused. (See also **damages**.)

complainant: Person who seeks to initiate court proceedings against another person. In a civil case, the complainant is the plaintiff; in a criminal case, the complainant is the state.

complaint: A written statement filed by the plaintiff that initiates a civil case, stating the wrongs allegedly committed by the defendant and requesting relief from the court. Sometimes called the initial pleading or petition.

concurrent sentences: Sentences served at the same time, e.g., concurrent sentences of ten years and five years equal a total of ten years served. (Compare **consecutive sentences**.)

confession: A statement by a person, either oral or written, admitting that he or she committed a certain offense.

conform copies: To receive or endorse file copies of an original document.

consecutive sentences: Two or more sentences served continuously, one right after another, e.g., consecutive sentences of ten years and five years equal a total of fifteen years served. (Compare **concurrent sentences**.)

conservatee: A person who is unable to care for himself or herself and who has a court-appointed caretaker. (See also **guardianship**.)

conservator: A person appointed by the court to take care of a conservatee and/or the property of one who is unable to care for himself or herself.

conservator of the estate: A person or organization appointed by a judge to manage the financial affairs of a person whom a judge has decided is unable to do so (the conservatee).

conservator of the person: A person or organization appointed by a judge to arrange for the personal care and protection of a person whom a judge has decided is unable to do so (the conservatee).

consolidation of actions: The grouping of multiple cases involving the same parties.

Constitution: The fundamental law of our nation that establishes the conception, character, and organization of its sovereign power and the manner of its exercise. Also, the document that contains the guiding rules and principles, the descriptions of the power of the government, and the essential rights of the people of a country or state or other governing collective.

contempt: An act or omission that obstructs the orderly administration of justice or impairs the dignity, respect, or authority of the court. May be demonstrated in behavior that shows intentional disregard or disobedience of a court order, either of which may be punishable by fine or imprisonment.

continuance: The postponement of an action pending in a court to a future date. (See also **adjournment** and **recess**.)

contract: (1) An agreement between two or more persons that creates an obligation to do or not to do a particular thing; (2) an agreement between two or more persons that creates, changes, or eliminates a legal relationship.

conviction: A judgment of guilt against a criminal defendant; the determination of guilt based on a plea, a jury verdict, or a finding of a judicial officer.

costs: (1) Certain fees and charges a party pays to file and present a case or to enforce a judgment; (2) an award of money for expenses in a civil suit.

count: Each distinct statement of a cause of action or charge

counterclaim: An independent cause of action by one party (either a plaintiff or a defendant) that opposes or offsets a previous claim made by the other party.

court: A judge or body of judges whose task is to hear cases and administer justice.

court order: A legally binding edict issued by a court of law. Can be issued by a magistrate, judge, or properly empowered administrative officer.

court reporter: A person who makes a word-for-word record of what is said in court, generally by using a stenographic machine, shorthand, or an audio recording device, and then produces a transcript of the proceedings upon request.

court stamp: An embossed seal press or stamp that prints or embosses a seal on court documents that will reproduce legibly in photocopies and may include the name of the judicial district or consolidated city and county upon it.

court trial: A trial without a jury in which a judicial officer determines both the issues of fact and the law in the case, sometimes referred to as bench trial.

crime: An act committed or omitted in violation of a law that forbids or commands it and which, upon conviction, results in a sentence of either one or a combination of the following punishments: (1) death; (2) imprisonment; (3) fine; (4) removal from office; (5) disqualification to hold and enjoy any office of honor, trust, or profit.

cross-claim/cross-complaint: A claim litigated by codefendant(s) or coplaintiff(s) against each other.

cross-defendant: The person named as the defendant in a cross-claim.

cross-examination: The testimony given by a witness when questioned by opposing counsel at a trial, hearing, or deposition.

custody: (1) Being under the restraint and physical control of the court to ensure appearance in court or the imprisonment of an accused after a criminal conviction; (2) the primary care and control of children.

custody order: Legally binding court order that establishes with whom a child shall live and who should make decisions about healthcare, education, and other key issues.

D

damages: An award of money paid by the losing party to the winning party to compensate for losses or injuries incurred. Can be compensatory, i.e., money paid as compensation for the actual cost of an injury or loss; or punitive/exemplary, i.e., an amount of money greater than the actual damages suffered that serves as punishment for willful or malicious acts by a defendant.

decedent: In criminal law, refers to the victim of a homicide; in probate matters, refers to a dead person.

declaration: In the law of evidence, a sworn statement evidencing, supporting, or establishing a fact in writing made by a person and which is certified or declared under penalty of perjury to be true and correct. All declarations must be dated and signed by the declarant (i.e., the person making the statement) and must show the place of execution and either name the state in which the document was executed or indicate that the declaration was made under the laws of the state in which the declaration is being filed.

decree: A court decision that can be either (1) interlocutory, i.e., a preliminary finding before final disposition, or (2) final, i.e., a final judgment in which all issues of a case are settled.

defamation: The offense of injuring a person's character, fame, or reputation by false and malicious unprotected statements.

default: The failure of a defendant to file an answer or appear in a civil case within the prescribed time after having been properly served with a summons and complaint.

default judgment: A judgment made in favor of the plaintiff because of the defendant's failure to answer or appear to contest the plaintiff's claim. (See also **vacate default judgment**.)

defendant: In a civil case, the person or organization against whom the plaintiff brings suit; in a criminal case, the person accused of the crime.

deliberations: The period during which a jury goes into the jury room to think about and discuss evidence and testimony to reach a verdict in a civil or criminal case.

delinquent: A minor who has committed an act that would be a crime if it were committed by an adult.

de novo: Trying a matter again as if it had not been heard before; from the Latin for "from new."

dependent: In family law, a person, usually a child, who is financially supported by another person. In juvenile law, a minor who is in the custody of the court because he or she has been abused, neglected, or molested or is physically dangerous to the public due to a mental or physical disorder.

deposition: Testimony, either written or oral, given under oath before an authorized third party. A deposition is given outside of court for the purpose of preserving testimony, or obtaining testimony from a witness living at a distance, and to aid in the preparation of pleadings. (See also **discovery**.)

dictum: A portion of a cited case that is relevant but not necessary to the case determination.

direct examination: Questioning of a witness in court by the party on whose behalf the witness was called to testify.

discovery: The gathering of information (facts, documents, or testimony) before a case goes to trial. Discovery may take the form of depositions, interrogatories, examinations, or admissions, or it can take place informally through independent investigation or conversations with opposing counsel.

dismiss with prejudice: To dismiss the present action and deny the right to file another suit on that claim.

dismiss without prejudice: To dismiss the present action but leave open the possibility of another suit on the same claim.

disposition: The final decision by the court in a controversy.

disqualification: Refers to the disqualification (usually voluntary) of a judge from hearing a case, generally based on any interest that may impair the judge's ability to decide the case in a fair and impartial manner.

dissolution: A marriage that is ended by a judge's decision. This is also known as a divorce. (Compare **nullity**.)

diversion: An alternative sentence (rather than jail) in which a defendant is supervised by a probation officer while attending a rehabilitation program so that upon successful completion the charges are dismissed without adjudication. (Compare **electronic surveillance, home detention**.)

divorce: A common name for a marriage that is legally dissolved.

docket: A log containing the complete history of each case in the form of brief chronological entries summarizing the court proceedings.

due process: The regular course of administration of law through the courts. A constitutional guarantee of due process requires that every person have the protection of a day in court, representation by an attorney, and the benefit of procedures that are speedy, fair, and impartial.

E

eminent domain: The right of the state to take private property for public use after providing fair compensation to the owner.

en banc: "On the bench" or "as a full bench." Refers to court sessions where the entire membership of a court participates rather than the usual number. U.S. circuit courts of appeals, for example, usually sit in panels of three judges, but all the judges in the court may decide certain matters together. They are then said to be sitting en banc (occasionally spelled "in banc").

enjoin: To command or require; to order that something be stopped.

equitable: (1) Describes civil suits in equity rather than in law. In English legal history, courts of law could order only the payment of damages. A separate court of equity could order someone to do something or to stop doing something. (See also **injunction**.) In American jurisprudence, the federal courts have both legal and equitable power, but the distinction is still important. For example, a trial by jury is normally available in law cases but not in equity cases. (2) To deal fairly and equally with all concerned. This implies not only a fair or just determination on legal grounds but also a judgment guided by common-sense notions of fairness and justice.

equity: A system supplemental to the law embodying principles of what is fair and right.

estoppel: An act or statement that precludes a person from later making claims to the contrary

et al.: The Latin phrase for "and others." Refers to additional parties not included in the formal name of a court case.

et ux.: The Latin phrase for "and wife."

evidence: Any type of proof that is legally presented at trial through witnesses, records, and/or exhibits.

executor: A person named in a will to carry out the will's directions and requests, usually under the supervision of the probate court. The executor's main responsibilities include taking care of the estate, paying the decedent's debts and estate taxes, and distributing the decedent's money and other property as directed by the will.

exhibit: A document or material object produced and identified in court for the purpose of introducing it as evidence in a case. Each of these documents or objects is ordinarily given an identifying letter or number in alphabetical or numerical sequence before it is offered as evidence.

exonerate: To clear from blame or to relieve from responsibility.

exonerate bail: Money or property returned by the court to the defendant or bondsman. (See also **bail exoneration**.)

ex parte: The Latin phrase for "from one side," e.g., *ex parte* hearings at which only one side in a lawsuit appears and argues the case.

expulsion: To force a student to leave school.

expunge: To strike out or erase.

extradition: The formal process of delivering a person apprehended in one state to the authorities of the state in which that person has been accused or convicted of a crime.

F

family law court: A type of court that hears matters related to dissolution of marriage, legal separation of spouses, nullification of marriage, child custody and support matters, and domestic violence petitions.

federal question jurisdiction: Jurisdiction given to federal courts in cases involving the interpretation and application of the U.S. Constitution, acts of Congress, and treaties.

felony: A criminal offense punishable by death or by imprisonment for more than one year.

fiduciary: A person who acts as a trustee or primarily for another person's benefit. As an adjective rather than a noun, fiduciary means something based on a trust or confidence. (See also **trustee**.)

finding: A determination of fact by a judicial officer or jury. (See also **settlement** and **verdict**.)

fine: A sum of money a person must pay as punishment because of an illegal act or omission.

foreperson: At the beginning of deliberations, the jury votes to select one of its members to be the foreperson. The jury foreperson's duty is to see that discussion during deliberations is carried on in a free and orderly manner, that the case and issues are fully and freely discussed, and that every juror is given a chance to participate in the discussion. As the deliberations conclude, the foreperson counts the votes and completes and signs the verdict form.

fraud: An intentional deception that financially injures another person(s) in any way. Usually strictly applied to specific elements (1) of representation of fact, (2) of false representation, (3) known to be false or recklessly indifferent, (4) where the intention is to have the victim change position, (5) where the victim changes position, (6) where the victim relies on representation, (7) in which representation is justified, (8) where the victim is damaged.

fugitive: A person who runs away or tries to escape custody.

full faith and credit: Doctrine under which a state must honor an order or judgment entered in another state.

G

garnishment: A legal process under which part of a person's wages and/or assets is withheld for payment of a debt. This term is usually used to specify that an income or wage withholding is involuntary.

grand jury: A body of sixteen to twenty-three citizens who listen to evidence of criminal allegations presented by prosecutors and determine whether there is probable cause to believe an individual committed an offense.

guarantor: One who promises to be responsible for the debt or default of another.

guardian *ad litem*: A court-appointed adult who represents a minor child or legally incompetent person. (See also ***ad litem*.**)

guardianship: A California court proceeding in which a judge appoints someone to care for a person under eighteen years of age or to manage the minor's estate, or both. In some states, conservatorship of an adult is called guardianship, but not in California.

H

habeas corpus: The name of a **writ** used to bring a person before a court or judge for determination of whether that person is being unlawfully denied his or her freedom; from the Latin for "you have the body."

hearsay: Statements by a witness who did not see or hear the incident in question but heard about it from someone else. Hearsay is usually not admissible as evidence in court.

home detention: Use of an electronic device to monitor the whereabouts and restrict the activities of a sentenced party in lieu of having the party serve time in jail.

homicide: The killing of one human being by the act, procurement, or omission of another (not necessarily a crime; see following). Can be (1) excusable, i.e., resulting from a lawful act when no hurt is intended or from an act of self-defense; (2) felonious, i.e., resulting from any wrongful act without any excuse or justification in law; or (3) justifiable, i.e., resulting from an intentional but lawful act such as the execution of a death sentence by an agent of the law (can also apply to self-defense).

I

immunity: A right of exception from duty or penalty. (See also **privilege**.)

impeachment: (1) The process of calling a witness's testimony into question. For example, if the attorney can show that the witness may have fabricated portions of his or her testimony, the witness is said to be "impeached"; (2) the constitutional process whereby the House of Representatives may "impeach" (accuse of misconduct) high officers of the federal government, who are then tried by the Senate.

impound: To seize and hold in the custody of the law; generally used in reference to objects or animals rather than people.

in camera: A hearing held in judge's chambers or in a court with all spectators excluded; from the Latin for "in chamber."

incarcerate: To confine to a jail.

incriminate: To hold another or oneself responsible for criminal misconduct.

indemnity: An obligation to provide compensation for a loss, injury, or damage.

indictment: The formal charge issued by a grand jury stating that there is enough evidence that the defendant committed the crime to justify having a trial; it is used primarily for felonies.

indigent: Generally, this term defines a person who is poor, needy, and has no one to look to for support.

in forma pauperis: Permission given by the court to a person to file a case without payment of the required court fees because the person cannot afford to pay them; from the Latin for "in the manner of a pauper."

information: A written accusation charging a person with a crime that is presented by a prosecuting officer under oath of office rather than produced by a grand jury.

infraction: A minor violation of a law, contract, or right that is not a misdemeanor or a felony and that cannot be punished by imprisonment.

injunction: A court order either prohibiting a defendant from performing a specific act or compelling a defendant to perform a specific act.

in limine: Latin for "at the beginning" or "at the threshold," such as a motion *in limine* at the beginning of trial to request that certain evidence be excluded.

in pro per: See *in propria persona.*

in propria persona: A case in which a party represents himself or herself without an attorney; abbreviated to "in pro per"; from the Latin for "in one's own proper person." See *pro se.*

inquest: A legal inquiry, before a court of law or other officers legally empowered to hold inquiries, usually to determine the cause and circumstances of a death.

instructions to jury: Instructions given by a judge to a jury immediately before they decide a case, telling the jury what laws apply to that case.

interpleader: When two or more persons assert a claim to the same thing held by a third party. The third party may compel them to go to trial with each other to arrive at a settlement.

interrogatories: Written questions sent by one party in a lawsuit to an opposing party as part of pretrial discovery in civil cases. The party receiving the interrogatories is required to answer them in writing under oath. (See also **discovery**.)

intestate: To die without making a will or leaving instructions for disposal of property after death. (See also **testate**.)

J

jeopardy: Danger to the defendant of possible conviction and punishment. In a criminal proceeding, the defendant is usually said to be "in jeopardy" after the jury has been sworn in and the preliminary hearing has taken place.

joinder: Generally, a coupling or joining together, e.g., plaintiffs joining in a suit or a joining of actions or defense.

judge: An official of the judicial branch with authority to decide lawsuits brought before courts. Used generically, the term "judge" may also refer to all judicial officers, including Supreme Court justices.

judgment: (1) The official decision of a court finally resolving the dispute between the parties to a lawsuit; (2) the official decision or finding of a judge or administrative agency hearing officer concerning the respective rights and claims of the parties to an action; also known as a **decree** or **order** and may include the findings of fact and conclusions of law; (3) the final decision of the judge stating which party has prevailed and the terms of the decision. Can be n.o.v. (from the Latin, ***non obstante veredicto***, for "notwithstanding the verdict"), i.e., a ruling in favor of one party despite the fact that there had been a verdict for the other party, or summary, i.e., court's decision prior to a trial directing that the action has no disputed facts and that one party is entitled to judgment as a matter of law.

judgment creditor: The party (either the plaintiff or the defendant) in whose favor a judgment has been awarded.

judgment debtor: (1) The party (either the plaintiff or the defendant on a defendant's claim) against whom the judgment has been entered; (2) the person who has been ordered by the court to make a money payment as a result of a civil suit.

jurisdiction: (1) The legal authority of a court to hear and decide a case; (2) the geographic area over which the court has authority to decide cases; (3) the territory, subject matter, or persons over which lawful authority may be exercised by a court, as determined by Constitution or statute.

jurisdictional limit: The maximum monetary amount that may be awarded by the court.

juror: A person selected to be on a jury.

jury: A group of citizens selected according to law and impaneled to determine the issues of fact in a case. Can be: (1) grand, i.e., body of citizens who determine whether probable cause exists that a crime has been committed and whether an indictment should be issued; (2) hung, i.e., a jury that is unable to agree on a verdict after a suitable period of deliberation; (3) petit (or trial), i.e., an ordinary jury for the trial of a criminal or civil action; or (4) special, i.e., a jury ordered by the court, on the motion of either party, in cases of unusual importance or intricacy.

juvenile: A person under the legal age of adulthood, usually eighteen years but in some instances twenty-one years.

juvenile court: That part of the superior court that has jurisdiction over delinquency, status offense, and dependency cases involving minors.

K

L

laches: Undue lapse of time in enforcing a right of action; negligence in failing to act more promptly.

lawsuit: (1) A legal action started by a plaintiff against a defendant based on a complaint that the defendant failed to perform a legal duty, which resulted in harm to the plaintiff; (2) a legal dispute brought to a court for resolution.

lease: An agreement for renting real property. A lease is usually written and for a set term, such as one year. A residential rental agreement can be oral and is presumed to be month-to-month.

legal separation: A married couple can end their relationship but still remain legally married and get court orders on parenting and money issues, with a judgment of legal separation.

levy: To raise, collect, or seize by legal process.

libel: False and malicious written, printed, or published material that is defamatory and injures the reputation of an individual. (Compare **slander**.)

lien: A claim upon property to prevent sale or transfer of that property until a debt is satisfied. The lien may be enforced or collected by levying on the property.

lis pendens: Jurisdiction of a court over property until final disposition; from the Latin for "a"pending suit."

litigants: The parties involved in a lawsuit.

litigate: To conduct or engage in a lawsuit.

litigation: A case, controversy, or lawsuit. Participants (plaintiffs and defendants) in lawsuits are called litigants.

long-arm jurisdiction: Legal provision that permits one state to claim personal jurisdiction over someone who lives in another state. There must be some meaningful connection between the person and the state or district that is asserting jurisdiction in order for a court or agency to reach beyond its normal jurisdictional border.

M

magistrate: A judicial officer having the power to issue arrest warrants and find probable cause at preliminary hearings.

malfeasance: Performance of an act that should not have been done at all. (Compare **misfeasance, nonfeasance**.)

manslaughter: The unlawful killing of a person without any deliberation. Can be voluntary, i.e., the unlawful taking of human life under circumstances falling short of premeditated intent to kill, or involuntary, i.e., the unintentional taking of human life as a result of performing an unlawful act or negligently performing a lawful act. (Compare **murder**; see also **homicide**.)

mayhem: Unlawfully and violently depriving a person of a member of his or her body or disabling, disfiguring, or rendering it useless (includes injury to eyes, tongue, nose, ears, etc.).

mediation: A process in which a neutral person or persons facilitate communication between disputants to assist them in reaching a mutually acceptable settlement.

minute order: An entry made by a court clerk to record a procedure or ruling in the courtroom. Also, an entry to record documents in the clerk's office.

minutes: The official (permanent) record of a court proceeding, e.g., what witnesses appeared, what motions were made, and what findings were reached.

misdemeanor: An offense punishable by one year of imprisonment or less.

misfeasance: Improper performance of an act that might have been lawfully done. (Compare **malfeasance, nonfeasance.**)

mistrial: A trial that has been terminated and declared void due to prejudicial error in the proceedings or other extraordinary circumstances.

moot: Open to debate, usually having no practical significance or relevance. A moot point is one not capable of being resolved by a judge, not disputed by either party, or one resolved out of court.

motion: An oral or written request made by a party to the court for a ruling or an order on a particular point. A motion to reduce bail is a request to decrease the amount of bail needed to guarantee that the defendant will appear in court when required. A motion to release on own recognizance is a request to release a defendant without bail, dependent upon agreement to appear when the court so orders. A motion to set is an application made to the judge to set a date for a future trial. A motion to quash is a request to make something void or ineffective, such as to quash a subpoena. (Compare **petition.**)

N

negligence: The failure of a person to use that degree of care in a given situation which by law one is obligated to use in order to protect the rights and property of others.

nolo contendere: No contest; from the Latin for "I do not wish to contend." A plea of *nolo contendere* has the same effect as a plea of guilty as far as the criminal sentence is concerned but may not be considered as an admission of guilt for any other purpose.

nonfeasance: Failure to perform an act for which one is legally responsible. (Compare **malfeasance, misfeasance**.)

notary public: A person authorized under civil law to administer oaths, to attest and certify that certain documents are authentic, and to take depositions.

nullity: The legal invalidation of a marriage; annulment. (Compare **dissolution**.)

nunc pro tunc: Used when an order is issued on one date but is effective retroactively; from the Latin for "now for then."

O

objection: A formal protest made by a party regarding testimony or evidence sought to be introduced by the other side.

obligee: The person, state agency, or other institution to which a debt such as child support is owed (also referred to as the custodial party when the money is owed to the person with primary custody of the child). (See also **support order**.)

obligor: The person who is obliged to pay child support or perform some other obligation. (See also **support order**.)

offset: Amount of money intercepted from a parent's state or federal income tax refund, or from an administrative payment such as federal retirement benefits, in order to satisfy a child-support debt.

opinion: A judge's written explanation of the decision of the court in appellate cases. Because a case may be heard by three or more judges in the court of appeals, the opinion in appellate decisions can take several forms. If all the judges completely agree on the result, one judge will write the opinion for all. If all the judges do not agree, the formal decision will be based upon the view of the majority, and one member of the majority will write the opinion. The judges who did not agree with the majority may write separately in dissenting or concurring opinions to present their views. A dissenting opinion disagrees with the majority opinion because of the reasoning and/or the principles of law the majority used to decide the case. A concurring opinion agrees with the decision of the majority opinion, but offers further comment or clarification or even an entirely different reason for reaching the same result. Only the majority opinion can serve as binding precedent in future cases. (See also **precedent**.)

oral argument: An opportunity for lawyers to summarize their position before the court and also to answer the judge's questions.

order: (1) Decision of a judicial officer; (2) a directive of the court, on a matter relating to the main proceedings, that decides a preliminary point or directs some steps in the proceedings. Generally used for invalidating a prior conviction, e.g., an order issued following a hearing in which a prior conviction is found invalid because certain legal standards were not met during the time of trial and conviction; setting a fee, e.g., an order directing a defendant to reimburse the county for costs incurred for a court-appointed attorney; to show cause, e.g., an order to appear in court to give reasons why an action cannot be carried out or should not have been or has not been carried out. (See also **court order, support order**.)

ordinance: A regulation established by a local government to enforce, control, or limit certain activities.

P

panel: (1) In appellate cases, a group of judges (usually three) assigned to decide the case; (2) in the jury selection process, the group of potential jurors; (3) the list of attorneys who are both available and qualified to serve as court-appointed counsel for criminal defendants who cannot afford their own counsel.

pardon: An act of grace by the chief executive of a state or country that releases a convicted person from punishment imposed by a court sentence.

parole: A conditional release from imprisonment that entitles the person receiving it to serve the remainder of the sentence outside of the prison as long as all conditions of release are met.

party: One of the litigants. At the trial level, the parties are typically referred to as the plaintiff or petitioner and the defendant or respondent. On appeal, they are known as the appellant and appellee.

paternity: Legal determination of fatherhood. Paternity must be established before a court can order child or medical support.

payee: Person or organization in whose name child support or other money is paid.

payor: Person who makes a payment.

***pendente lite*:** Describes orders made during the actual progress of the lawsuit prior to final disposition; from the Latin for "during the suit."

peremptory challenge: A challenge, by either the defense attorney or the prosecuting attorney, of a potential juror that usually results in that person's disqualification from jury service and does not require a stated reason for why the challenge is made. The number of peremptory challenges is prescribed by statute. (Compare **challenge for cause**.)

perjury: A false statement made willfully and knowingly while under oath in a court proceeding.

personal injury: A kind of civil case that includes actions for damages for physical injury to persons and property and actions for wrongful death.

personal jurisdiction: The power of a court over the person of a defendant in contrast to the jurisdiction of a court over the property of a defendant.

personal service: Service of court papers by handing a copy to the person who is served. (See also **process server**.)

petit jury: Also called "trial jury," a group of citizens who hear the evidence presented by both sides at trial and determine the facts in dispute. Criminal juries consist of twelve persons in federal court; civil juries consist of at least six persons. (See also **jury** and **grand jury**.)

petition: A formal written request presented to the court requesting specific judicial action. (Compare **motion**.)

petitioner: One who presents a petition to the court.

plaintiff: A person who brings an action; the party who complains or sues in a civil case.

plea: In a criminal case, the defendant's statement pleading "guilty" or "not guilty" in answer to the charges. (See also ***nolo contendere***.)

plea bargain: Negotiation between the prosecutor and the accused to exchange a guilty plea for conviction of a lesser charge, subject to approval by the court.

pleading: (1) Written statement filed with the court that describes a party's legal or factual assertions about the case; (2) a written statement in which one party responds to another's allegations to narrow the dispute to one or more specific points of difference.

polling of jury: A practice in which jurors are asked individually whether they concur with the verdict as rendered.

power of attorney: A person (the "principal") authorizes someone else (the "agent" or "attorney in fact") to take care of business for the principal. A power of attorney authorizes the agent to do whatever is necessary to manage the principal's assets. A limited or special power of attorney can be drawn up to be more restrictive, by setting time limits for the agent to serve, limiting the agent to particular actions, or authorizing the agent to manage just particular assets. There are general powers of attorney, limited or special powers of attorney, and durable powers of attorney. A general or limited power of attorney ends when the principal becomes incompetent. A durable power of attorney stays in effect if the principal becomes incapacitated.

precedent: A court decision in an earlier case with facts and legal issues similar to a dispute currently before a court. Judges will generally follow precedent, meaning that they use the principles established in earlier cases to decide new cases dealing with similar facts and legal issues. A judge will disregard precedent if a party can show that the earlier case was wrongly decided or that it differed in some significant way from the current case.

preliminary examination/hearing: A proceeding before a judicial officer in which evidence is presented so that the court can determine whether there is sufficient cause to hold the accused for trial on a felony charge.

presentence report: A report prepared by the probation department for the judge's reference when sentencing a defendant. Describes defendant's background: financial, job, and family status; community ties; criminal history; and facts of the current offense. A presentence report is required in felony cases but may or may not be requested in misdemeanor cases.

presiding judge/justice: In a court with multiple judicial officers, the judge/justice who performs the basic administrative functions of managing the court's business.

pretrial conference: A meeting of the judge and lawyers to plan the trial, discuss which matters should be presented to the jury, review proposed evidence and witnesses, and set a trial schedule. Typically, the judge and the lawyers also discuss the possibility of settling the case.

prima facie: Not requiring further support to establish existence, credibility, or validity; from the Latin for "from first view." A prima facie case is sufficient on its face because it is supported by the necessary minimum evidence and free from obvious defects. Prima facie evidence is sufficient to support a certain conclusion unless contradictory evidence is presented.

privilege: An advantage not enjoyed by all; a special exemption from prosecution or other lawsuits. (See also **immunity**.)

probable cause: A reasonable basis for assuming that a charge or fact is well founded.

probate: The judicial process in which a document purporting to be the will of a deceased person is proved to be genuine or not; lawful distribution of a decedent's estate.

probate court: The department of each county's superior court that deals with probate conservatorships, guardianships, and the estates of people who have died.

probation: (1) A sentencing alternative to imprisonment in which the court releases a convicted defendant under supervision of a probation officer who makes certain that the defendant follows certain rules, e.g., gets a job, gets drug counseling; (2) a department of the court that prepares a presentence report.

probation officer: Officers of the probation department of a court. A probation officer's duties include conducting presentence investigations, preparing presentence reports on convicted defendants, and supervising released defendants.

probation report: (See also **presentence report.**)

pro bono: Legal services performed for free; from the Latin meaning "for the good."

process: A course of proceedings in a lawsuit. Process also can mean a legal document that compels a defendant to answer a complaint filed or to accept a default judgment.

process server: A person who serves court papers on a party to a suit. (See also **personal service, service of process, substituted service.**)

promissory note: A written document by which one person promises to pay money to another.

pronouncement of judgment: The formal issuance by the judge of a judgment in a case.

proof: Evidence that tends to establish the existence of a fact at issue.

proof of service: The form filed with the court that proves the date on which documents were formally served on a party in a court action.

pro se: Refers to persons who present their own cases without lawyers; from the Latin for "on one's own behalf." (See also ***in propria persona.***)

prosecute: To charge someone with a crime and then try that person for it. A prosecutor tries a criminal case on behalf of the government.

prosecuting attorney: A public officer that prosecutes criminal cases on behalf of the citizenry; sometimes referred to as district attorney.

pro tem judge: An attorney who volunteers his or her time to hear and decide cases. Also called a temporary judge.

pro tempore judge: A referee or commissioner sitting temporarily and provisionally for a judge; same as pro tem judge; from the Latin for "for the time being" or "temporarily."

proximate cause: That which in natural and continuous sequence, unbroken by any independent cause, produces an event without which an injury would not have occurred.

public defender: Counsel appointed by the court, primarily to defend indigent defendants in criminal cases.

Q

Qualified Domestic Relations Order (QDRO): An order, decree, or judgment, including approval of a settlement agreement issued by a court and approved by a pension plan, that provides for division of a pension plan to make an equitable property division or payment of child or spousal support.

quash: To make void; to vacate; to annul; to set aside.

quiet title: An action in which the ownership of certain land is in dispute and submitted to the court for determination. To quiet title is to declare that a certain person is the rightful owner of the real property in dispute.

R

rebuttal: Evidence presented at trial by one party intended to overcome evidence introduced by another party.

recess: A brief adjournment in a trial ordered by the judge. (See also **adjournment**; compare **continuance**.)

recidivist: Habitual criminal.

reciprocity: A relationship in which one state grants certain privileges to other states or the citizens of other states on the condition that it or its citizens receive the same privilege.

record: A written account of the proceedings in a case, including all pleadings, evidence, and exhibits submitted in the course of the case.

record on appeal: A copy of the pleadings, exhibits, orders, or decrees filed in a case in a trial court as well as a transcript of the testimony taken in the case.

recuse: To excuse (oneself) or be excused from a criminal or civil proceeding because of conflict of interest. For example, a judge may recuse himself or herself from a small claims case because of personal or professional involvement with one or more of the parties.

referee: A person appointed by the court to hear and make decisions on certain limited legal matters, e.g., juvenile or traffic offenses.

remand: (1) The act of an appellate court sending a case to a lower court for further proceedings; (2) to return a prisoner to custody.

remittitur (of record): The transfer of the records of a case from a court of appeal to the original trial court for further action or other disposition as ordered by the appellate court.

request for admission: A method of discovery in which one party formally and in writing asks the opposing party to admit the truth of certain facts relevant to a case. (See also **discovery**.)

respondent: The person against whom an appeal is made; the responding party in a dissolution, nullity, adoption, or probate matter. (See also **dissolution, nullity**.)

restitution: The act of restoring or giving the equivalent value to compensate for an injury, damage, or loss.

restraining order: A time-limited court order that directs a person to stop doing something until a formal hearing is held to determine an outcome. (See also **injunction**.)

reverse: When an appellate court sets aside the decision of a trial court. A reversal is often accompanied by a remand to the lower court for further proceedings.

S

sanction: (1) To concur, confirm, or ratify. (2) A penalty or punishment to enforce obedience to the law.

satisfaction: Payment of a judgment amount by the losing party.

sealed record: A record closed by a court to further inspection by anyone unless further ordered by the court.

sentence: The formal pronouncement by a court stating the punishment to be imposed on a person convicted of a criminal offense.

sentencing guidelines: A set of rules and principles established by the United States Sentencing Commission that trial judges use to determine the sentence in a federal case for a convicted defendant.

sequestration: A sequestered jury is usually housed together in a hotel and prohibited from contacting people outside of the court. Sequestration rarely occurs and is meant for jurors' protection. It is used to keep the jurors away from the media during a controversial trial where widespread media coverage could influence a juror's decision. In rare cases, there may be attempts to influence the jurors' deliberation through threats.

service by publication: Service of process accomplished by publishing a notice in a newspaper or by posting on a bulletin board of a courthouse or other public facility after a court determines that other means of service are impractical or have been unsuccessful. (See also **service of process**.)

service of process: The delivery of legal documents to the opposing party completed by an adult over the age of eighteen who is not a party to the action who swears to the date and method of delivery to the recipient. (See also **personal service, substituted service**.)

settlement: An agreement reached among the parties that resolves the case at any time before court findings or a jury verdict. (See also **finding, verdict**.)

severance of actions: To separate multiple criminal actions, defendants, causes of action, or cross-complaints for separate trials.

show cause: A court order directing a person to appear in court and present any evidence why the remedies stated in the order should not be confirmed or executed. A show cause order is usually based on a motion and affidavit asking for the judge to make certain decisions.

sine die: Without assigning a specific day for further hearing; from the Latin for "without a day."

slander: Defamation of a person's character or reputation through false or malicious oral statements. (Compare **libel.**)

spousal support: Court-ordered support of a spouse or ex-spouse; also referred to as maintenance or alimony.

statute: A law passed by Congress or a state legislature.

statute of limitations: A law that sets the deadline by which parties must file suit to enforce their rights.

stay order: An order issued by a court halting court proceedings until a further event takes place.

stipulation: An agreement relating to a pending court proceeding between parties or their attorneys.

strike: To delete or remove, as in to strike (a case) from the court's calendar.

sua sponte: Commonly used to describe when a judge does something without being so requested by either party in a case; from the Latin for "of one's own will."

subpoena: An official order to attend court at a stated time. The most common use of the subpoena is to summon witnesses to court for the purpose of testifying in a trial.

subpoena duces tecum: An official order to produce documents or records at a stated place and time.

subrogation: To substitute one person in place of another with reference to a legal claim; for instance, an insurance company paying a victim's medical expenses would be able to collect those sums from the party causing the injury under the doctrine of subrogation.

substituted service: Service of process on a party by leaving the court papers with someone other than a party to the lawsuit; valid only if certain specified procedures are followed. (See also **service of process.**)

summary judgment: A court decision made on the basis of statements and evidence presented for the record without a trial. It is used when there are no factual disputes to resolve in the case. Summary judgment is granted when, on the undisputed facts in the record, a party is entitled to judgment in its favor as a matter of law.

summons: A notice to a defendant that an action against him or her has been commenced in the court issuing the summons and that a judgment will be taken against him or her if the complaint is not answered within a certain time.

support order: A judgment, decree, or order issued by a court for the support and maintenance of a child or spouse. This includes a child who has attained the age of majority under the law of the issuing state or that of the parent with whom the child is living. Support orders can incorporate the provision of monetary support, healthcare, payment of arrearages, or reimbursement of court costs and attorney fees, interest and penalties, and other forms of relief. (See also **obligation, obligor.**)

suppress: To stop or put an end to someone's activities. To suppress evidence is to withhold it from disclosure or publication.

surety bond: An insurance policy taken out by a defendant with a national insurance company in which the company agrees to pay the county the amount of bail required for the defendant's release should the defendant fail to make court appearances.

suspend: To postpone, stay, or withhold certain conditions of a judicial sentence for a temporary period of time.

suspended sentence: In criminal law, this means, in effect, that the defendant is not required at the time the sentence is imposed to serve the sentence.

T

temporary restraining order: A court order that prohibits a person from taking any action that is likely to cause irreparable harm. This differs from an injunction in that it may be granted immediately, without notice to the opposing party and without a hearing. It is intended to last only until a hearing can be held. Sometimes referred to as a TRO. Often used in domestic violence cases to prohibit further violence or threat of violence.

tenancy at will: A right to occupy property for an indefinite term that is created by the owner or person in lawful possession giving permission to another person to occupy the property. Terminating a tenancy at will requires the same legal procedure as terminating a month-to-month tenancy. (See **lease.**)

tenant: A person who rents property.

testate: Having made a will or having died leaving a valid will. (See also **intestate.**)

testator: A person who has made a will or who has died leaving a valid will.

testify: To give evidence under oath as a witness in a judicial proceeding.

testimony: Evidence presented orally by witnesses during trials, before grand juries, or during administrative proceedings.

third-party action: Generally, an action taken by anyone who is not a party to an underlying contract, agreement, or other transaction.

toll: See **statute of limitations.**

tort: A private or civil wrong, independent of contract; failure to perform some duty imposed by law or custom, resulting in injury to another. The victim of a tort may be entitled to sue for damages to compensate for the harm suffered. Victims of crimes may also sue in tort for the wrongs done to them. (See also **damages.**)

tortfeasor: A person who commits or is found guilty of a tort.

transcript: A written, word-for-word record of what was said, either in a proceeding such as a trial or during some other formal conversation such as a hearing or oral deposition.

trial: The hearing and determination of issues of fact and law, in accordance with prescribed legal procedures, in order to reach a disposition. Can be either (1) a bench trial, i.e., a court trial that is heard and decided by a judge, or (2) a jury trial, i.e., a court trial that is heard and decided by a jury, which usually consists of twelve people.

trial court: The first court to consider litigation, generally the superior court. (Compare **appellate court**.)

tribunal: A court, administrative agency, or quasi-judicial agency authorized to establish or modify support orders or to determine parentage.

trustee: (1) The person who has custody of or control over funds or items for the benefit of another; (2) in a bankruptcy case, a person appointed to represent the interests of the bankruptcy estate and the unsecured creditors. The trustee's responsibilities may include liquidating the property of the estate, making distributions to creditors, and bringing actions against creditors or the debtor to recover property of the bankruptcy estate.

U

U.S. attorney: A lawyer appointed by the president in each judicial district to prosecute and defend cases for the federal government. The U.S. attorney employs a staff of assistant U.S. attorneys who appear as the government's attorneys in individual cases.

unlawful detainer: A person who detains or continues to hold some real property that is no longer rightfully his or hers. An unlawful detainer is also the name for a summary civil action in which a landlord seeks to evict a tenant who the landlord claims is no longer entitled to live on the premises.

uphold: To agree by an appellate court with the lower court's decision and to allow it to stand. (See also **affirmation**.)

V

vacate the default judgment: Get a default judgment removed or erased. (See also **default judgment**.)

venire: Most commonly used to describe the whole group of people called for jury duty from which the jurors are selected. From the Latin for "to come" (as in to come, or appear, before the court).

venue: The particular court in which an action may properly be brought.

verdict: The decision of a trial jury or a judge that determines the guilt or innocence of a criminal defendant or that determines the final outcome of a civil case. Can be: (1) general, i.e., a verdict given in a civil case in which the jury finds in favor of the plaintiff or in favor of the defendant; (2) special/directed, i.e., a verdict given by the judge in a civil case, after considering the law as it applies to the case and after the jury states its conclusions on specific factual issues. (See also **finding, settlement.**)

verification: An oral or written statement that something is true, usually sworn to under oath.

voir dire: The process by which judges and lawyers select a trial jury from among those eligible to serve by questioning them to make certain that they can fairly decide the case; from the French for "to see and to speak."

W

wage assignment: A voluntary agreement by an employee to transfer (or assign) portions of future wage payments to pay certain debts, such as child support.

wage attachment: An involuntary transfer of a portion of an employee's wage payment to satisfy a debt.

wage garnishment: A legal procedure that requires the employer of a judgment debtor to withhold a portion of the judgment debtor's wages to satisfy a judgment.

waiver: To give up a legal right voluntarily, intentionally, and with full knowledge of the consequences.

ward of the court: A minor who is under the care and control of the juvenile court rather than his or her parent(s).

warrant: A written order issued and signed by a judicial officer directing a peace officer to take specific action. Can be: (1) an arrest warrant, i.e., one that commands a peace officer to arrest and bring before the court the person accused of an offense for purpose of commencing legal action; (2) a bench warrant, i.e., a written order issued by the court from the judge or bench commanding a person's arrest because of his or her failure to appear in court; (3) a recall warrant, i.e., a procedure for removing from police computers information concerning canceled warrants in order to avoid mistaken arrests; or (4) a search warrant, i.e., an order issued by a judge, based on a finding of probable cause, directing law enforcement officers to conduct a search of specific premises for specific persons or things and to bring them before the court.

warranty of habitability: A promise that goes with the rental of residential property that it will be fit for human habitation, including working plumbing and electrical systems, locking doors and windows, watertight roof, and other health and safety conditions. This promise is by statute, even if the landlord does not include it in the lease or rental agreement.

will: The written instrument by which a person declares his or her wishes about the disposition of personal property after death.

without prejudice: A term used when rights or privileges are not waived or lost. A dismissal of a lawsuit without prejudice allows a new suit to be brought on the same cause of action so long as it is within the statute of limitations.

witness: A person called by either side in a lawsuit to give testimony before the court or jury.

writ: A written order or directive issued by a court commanding that certain action be taken. Can be a writ of: (1) attachment, i.e., one that orders that specified property be attached; (2) certiorari, i.e., an order by an appellate court granting or denying a review of judgment; (3) execution, i.e., an order directing the enforcement of a court judgment; (4) habeas corpus, i.e., a writ that orders the release of someone who has been unlawfully imprisoned; (5) mandamus (or mandate), i.e., a writ that orders the performance of any act designated by law to be part of a person's duty or status; or (6) prohibition, i.e., the counterpart of a writ of mandate that orders that further proceedings or other official acts be stopped (usually issued from a higher to a lower court).

writ of certiorari: An order issued by the U.S. Supreme Court directing a lower court to transmit records for a case that the Supreme Court will hear on appeal.

About the Authors

John C. Peick is a principal in the firm of Peick Conniff, P.S. and practices law from offices in Bellevue, Washington. Mr. Peick practices in the areas of healthcare/business law with an emphasis on healthcare providers and clinics, and serious personal injury or wrongful death claims (excluding medical malpractice.)

He is a graduate of the University of Washington with a BA in political science in 1972. He attended the University of Iowa School of Law in Iowa City, Iowa, transferred to the UW Law School in 1973, and graduated in 1975 with a juris doctor (JD) degree. He is a member of the Washington State Bar Association (1975), U.S. District Court, Western District, Washington (1975), U.S. Tax Court (1976), and Ninth Circuit Court of Appeals (1998). He is a member of the Washington State Bar Association, American Bar Association, American Health Lawyers Association, Washington State Trial Lawyers Association, American Trial Lawyers Association, and National Association of Chiropractic Attorneys.

He has taught law courses on the community- and four-year-college level and been a frequent speaker at various healthcare provider seminars or meetings, as well as a speaker at legal professional seminars. He regularly contributes articles on regulatory compliance and other legal healthcare issues to local healthcare provider publications. You may email Mr. Peick at jpeick@peickconniff.com or call at 425-462-0660.

David Matteson has, for over twenty-five years, explored the nature of ideas and their expression, innovations in the marketplace, and relationships between people, public policy, and social systems. From this macro worldview, he has helped dozens of executive teams, non-profit boards, and business leaders manifest their visions and ideas into practical, clear, real-world actions. His work has helped them define their objectives, design action steps to obtain them, and successfully execute their plans. He has a well-earned reputation for building bridges of trust and designing business solutions for and between groups with diverse interests.

Matteson acts as a consultant to provide innovative dispute resolution and facilitated decision-making services to businesses whose products and services triggered public debate. Today, Matteson provides his clients a sophisticated boutique consulting practice, offering an array of services in executive leadership, business start-up and development, corporate and marketing communications, and issues management. Matteson's ability to develop integral solutions, creatively combining multiple business dynamics, makes the firm's services uniquely valuable in pursuing unprecedented opportunities and resolving complex problems.

Mr. Matteson is uniquely qualified to accomplish these business leadership and sophisticated communications tasks. He has held several senior management and executive corporate positions, mediated and facilitated numerous complex issue processes, and been personal advisor to many senior executives. In addition to his undergraduate degrees in environmental biology and civil engineering from Union College in New York, he holds three advanced degrees: a Master of Public Health and a Master of Public Policy from the University of Hawaii, as well as a Master of Science in Education from the State University of New York at Albany. Additionally, he is a certified mediator and trainer and is accredited in public relations.

You may email Mr. Matteson at matteson@earlyedgesolutions.com, find his website at http://www.earlyedgesolutions.com, or call at 425-670-2254.